Taylor Swift
FEARLESS

ISBN 978-1-4234-7841-6

HAL•LEONARD®
CORPORATION

7777 W. BLUEMOUND RD. P.O. BOX 13819 MILWAUKEE, WI 53213

Visit Hal Leonard Online at
www.halleonard.com

FEARLESS

Words and Music by TAYLOR SWIFT,
LIZ ROSE and HILLARY LINDSEY

Moderately

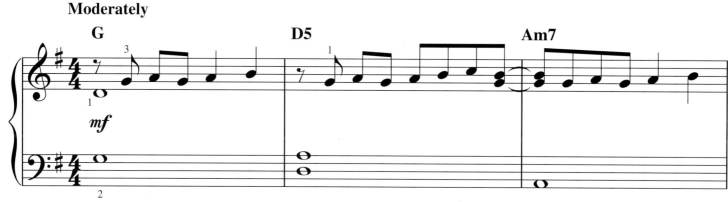

With pedal

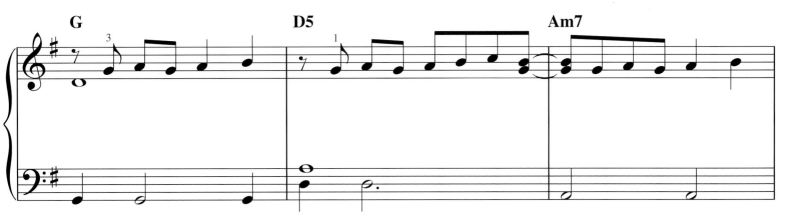

We're driv-in' down the road.   I won-der if you

know I'm try-in' so hard   not to get caught up   now. ___   But you're just so   cool,

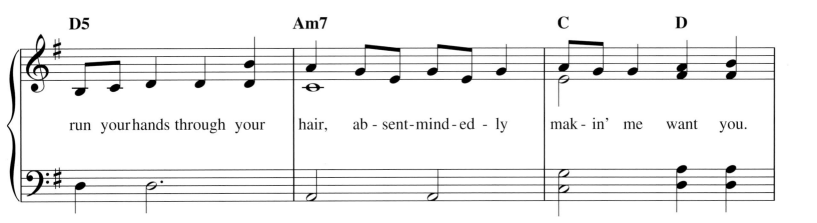

run your hands through your   hair,   ab-sent-mind-ed-ly   mak-in' me   want   you.

8

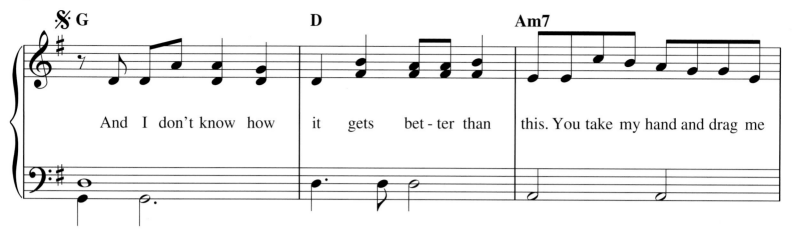

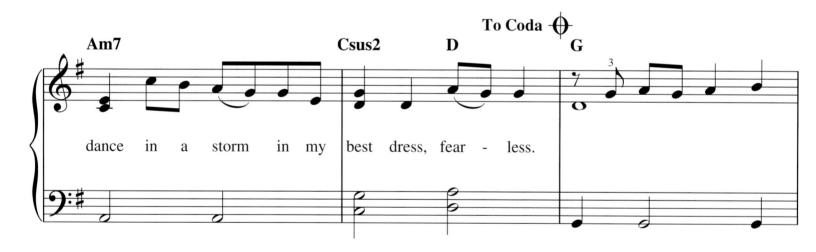

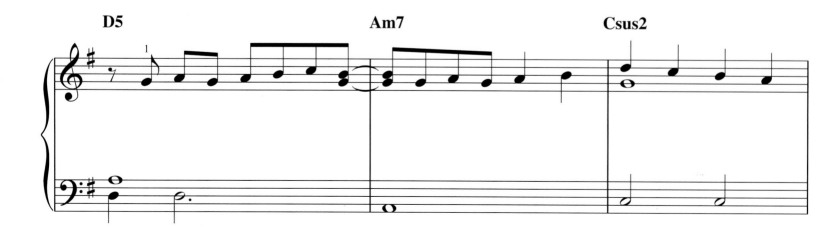

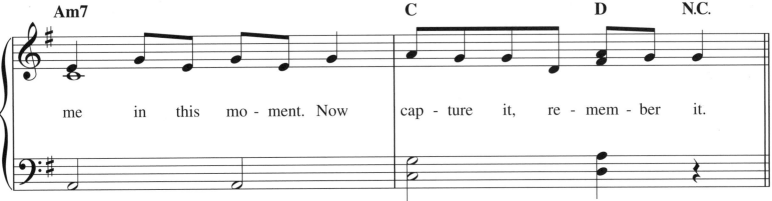

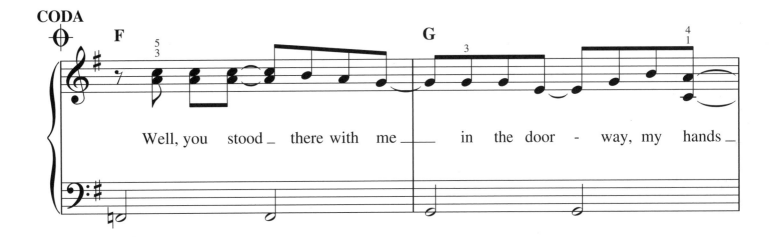

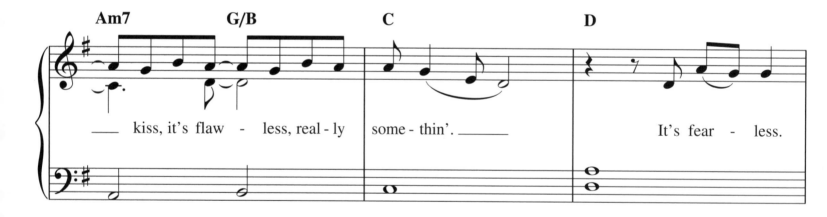

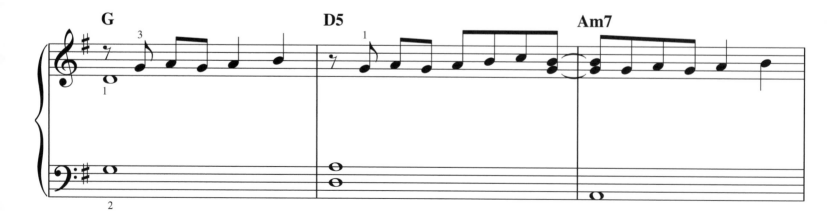

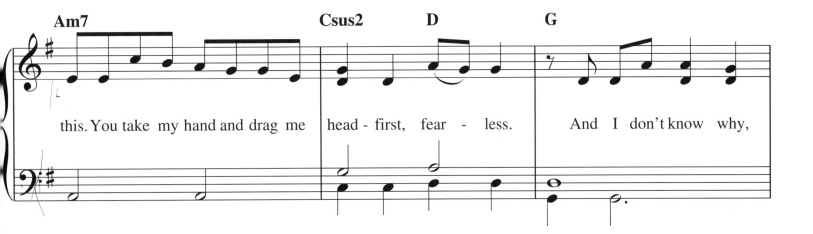

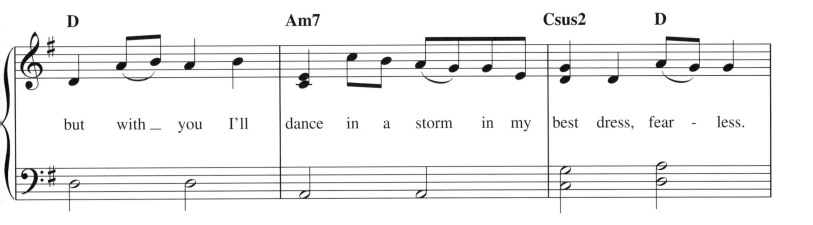

FIFTEEN

Words and Music by
TAYLOR SWIFT

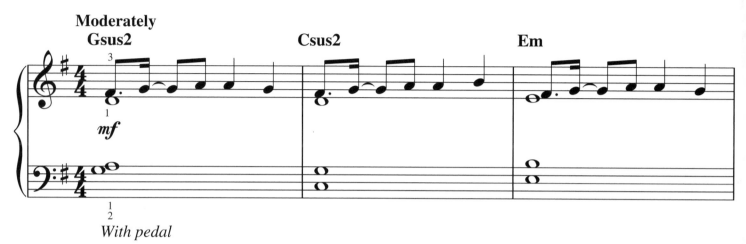

1. You take a deep breath and you walk through the doors. __ It's the morn-
2. (See additional lyrics)

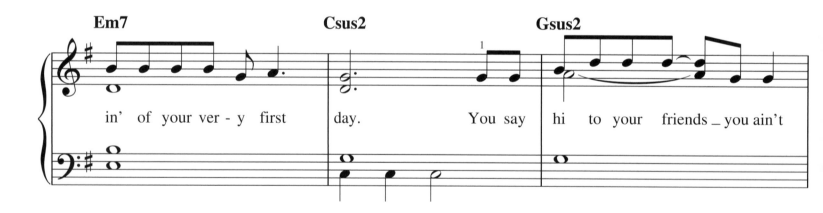

in' of your ver-y first day. You say hi to your friends __ you ain't

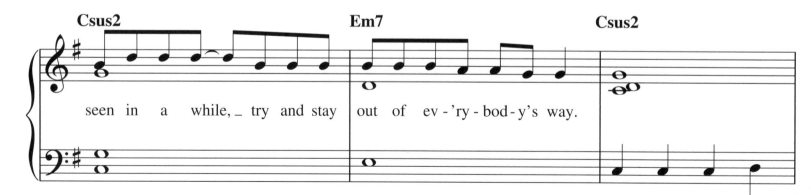

seen in a while, __ try and stay out of ev-'ry-bod-y's way.

It's your fresh - man year and you're gon - na be here ___ for the

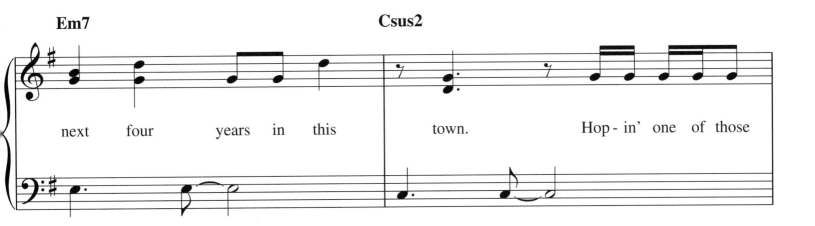

next four years in this town. Hop - in' one of those

sen-ior boys ___ will wink at you and say, "You know, I have-n't seen you a - round ___

___ be - fore." ___ 'Cause when you're fif - teen

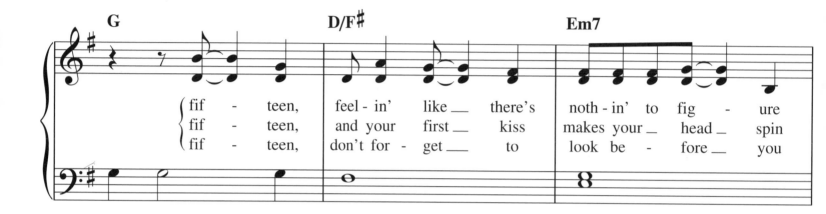

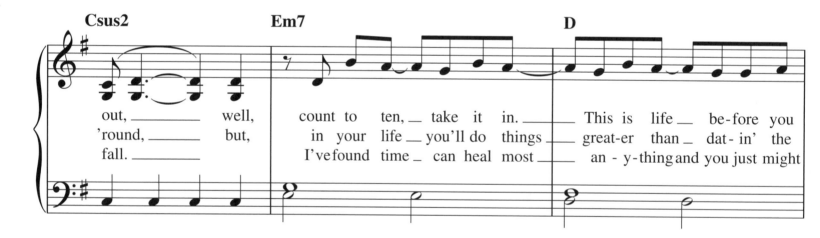

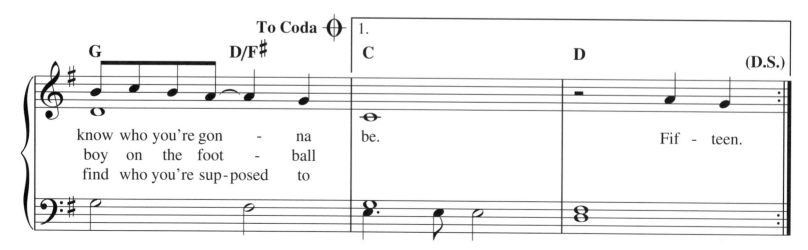

15

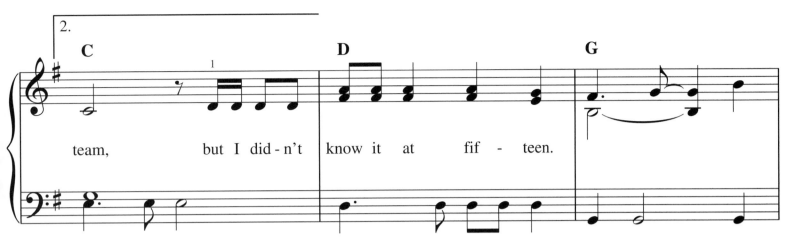

team, but I did-n't know it at fif - teen.

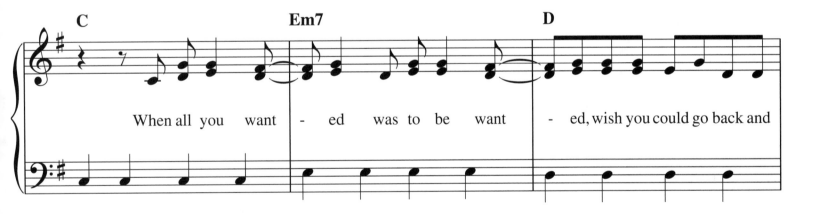

When all you want - ed was to be want - ed, wish you could go back and

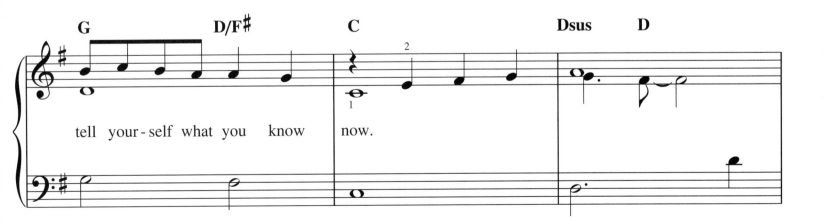

tell your-self what you know now.

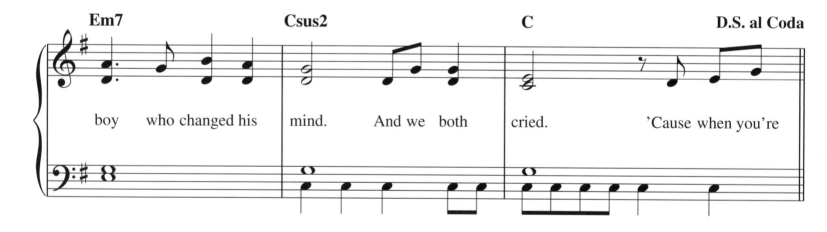

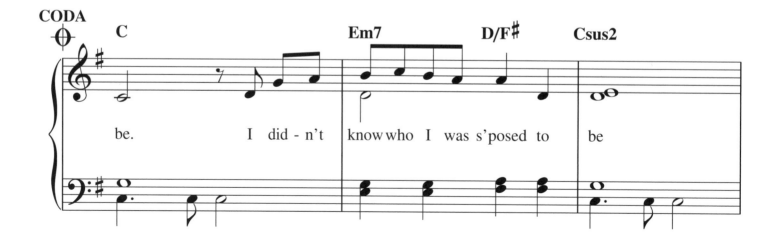

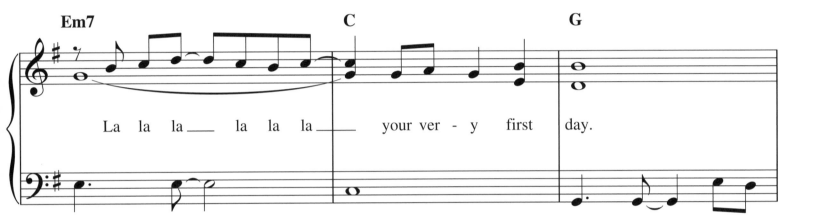

Additional Lyrics

2. You sit in class next to a redhead named Abigail
   And soon enough you're best friends,
   Laughin' at the other girls who think they're so cool.
   We'll be out of here as soon as we can.
   And then you're on your very first date
   And he's got a car and you feel like flyin'.
   And you're mama's waitin' up and you're thinkin' he's the one
   And you're dancin' 'round your room when the night ends.
   Chorus

LOVE STORY

Words and Music by
TAYLOR SWIFT

We were both young when

I first saw ___ you. I close my eyes ___ and the flash-back starts. ___ I'm stand-in'

there ..... on a bal - co - ny in sum-mer air. _____

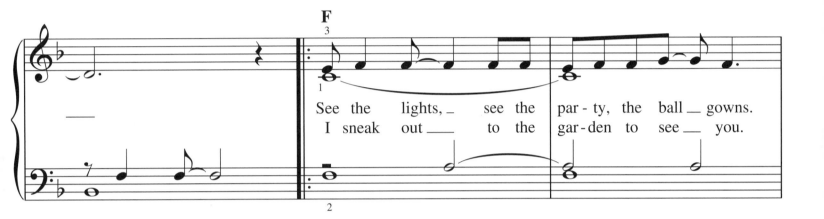

_____ See the lights, _ see the par - ty, the ball _ gowns.
I sneak out _____ to the gar - den to see _ you.

See you make _ your way through the crowd _ and say hel - lo.
We keep quiet _ 'cause we're dead if they knew. So, close your eyes,

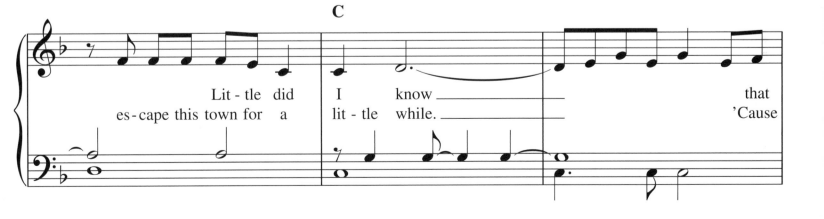

Lit - tle did I know _____ that
es - cape this town for a lit - tle while. _____ 'Cause

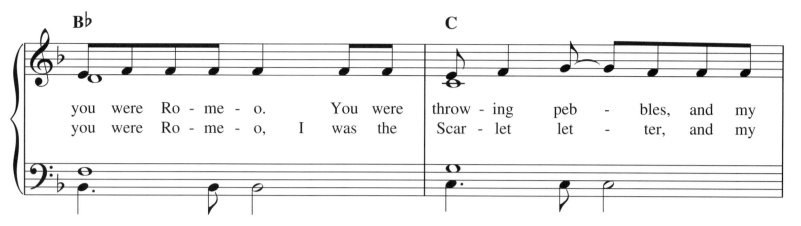

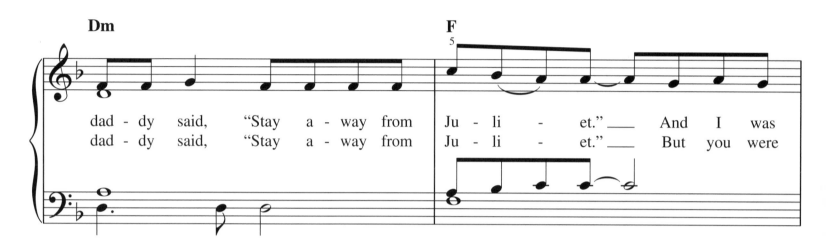

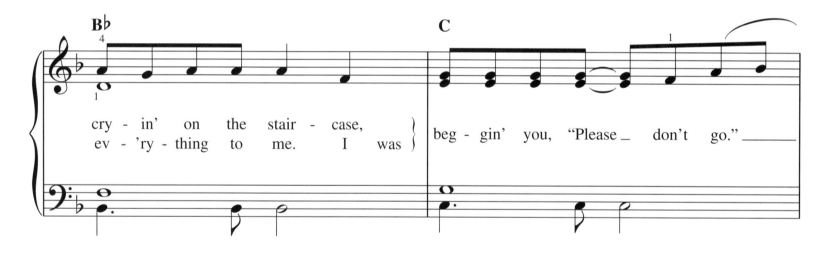

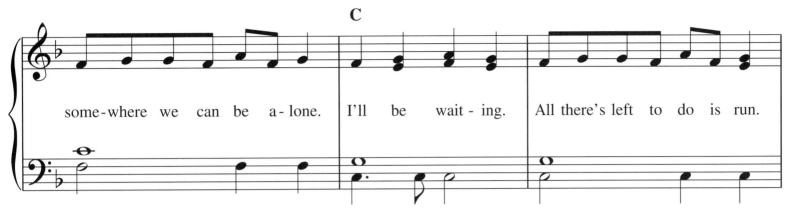

some-where we can be a-lone. I'll be wait-ing. All there's left to do is run.

You'll be the prince and I'll be the prin - cess. It's a love sto - ry. ___

Ba - by, just say __ yes." So

"Ro - me - o, save me. They're try'n' to tell me how to feel. This love is dif - fi - cult,

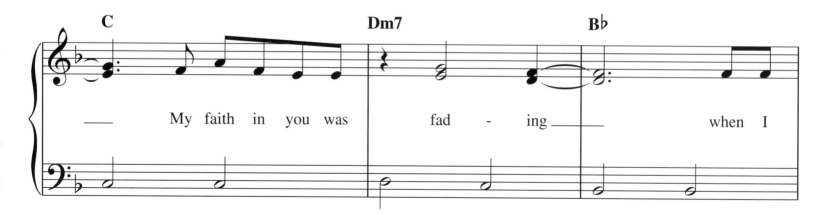

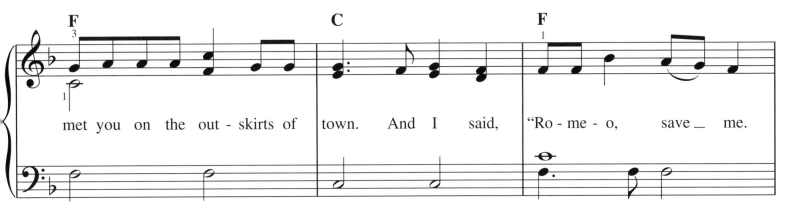

met you on the out - skirts of town. And I said, "Ro - me - o, save _ me.

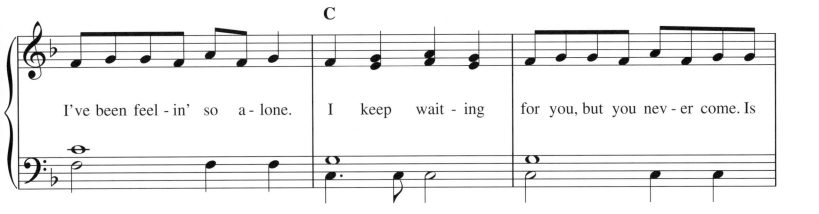

I've been feel - in' so a - lone. I keep wait - ing for you, but you nev - er come. Is

this in my head? I don't know what to think." He knelt to the ground and

pulled out a ring and said, "Mar - ry me, Ju - li - et, you nev - er have to be a - lone.

I love you __ and that's all I real-ly know. I talked to your dad. Go

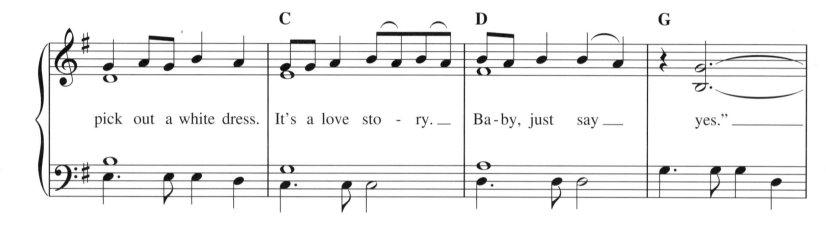

pick out a white dress. It's a love sto - ry. __ Ba - by, just say __ yes." __

__ Oh, oh, oh, __ oh, oh, oh, oh.

'Cause we were both young when I first saw __ you.

HEY STEPHEN

Words and Music by
TAYLOR SWIFT

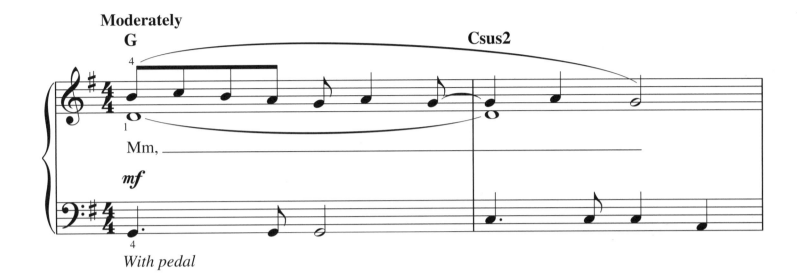

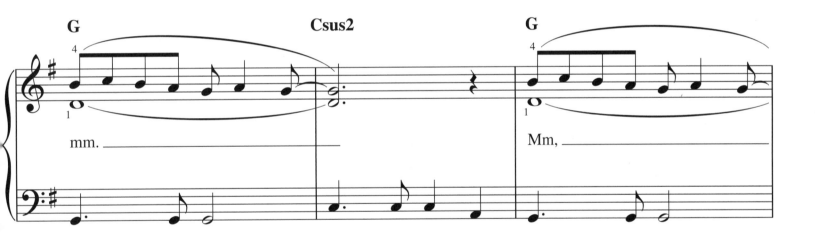

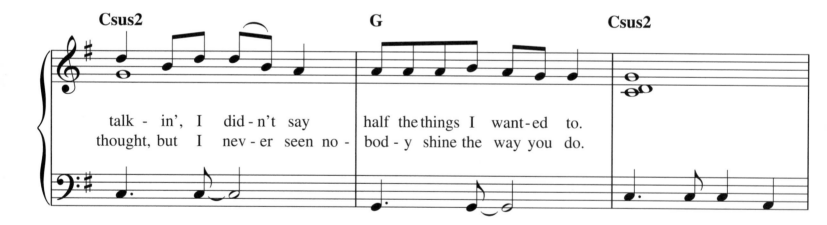

there   e - ven when it's cold.
ful,   don't you   ev - er   change.

Hey,   Steph - en, boy, you
Hey,   Steph - en, why are

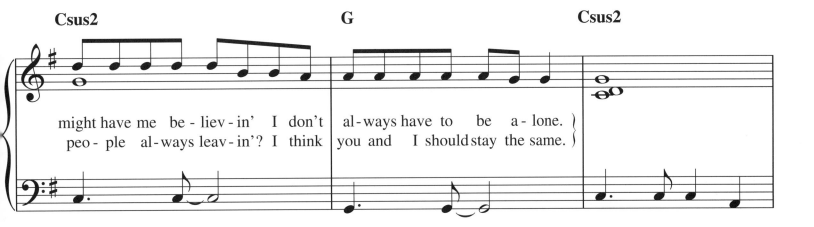

might have me be - liev - in' I don't
peo - ple al - ways leav - in'? I think

al - ways have to   be   a - lone.
you and   I should stay the same.

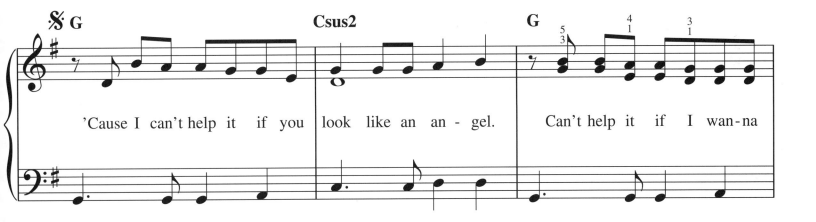

'Cause I can't help it if you

look like an an - gel.

Can't help it if I wan - na

kiss you in the rain. So,

come feel this mag - ic I've been

feel - in' since I met you.   Can't

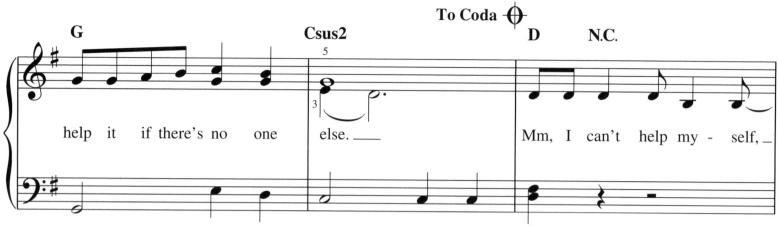

help it if there's no one else. ____ Mm, I can't help my-self, __

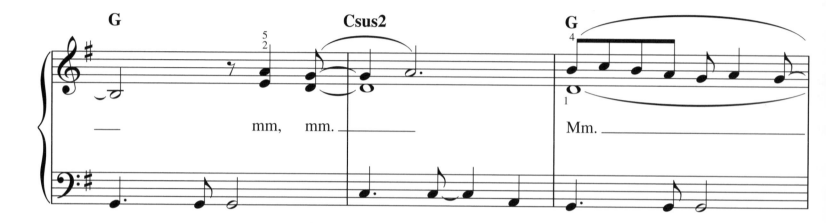

__ mm, mm. Mm. _____

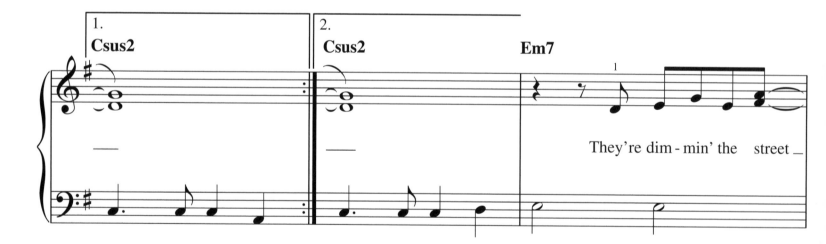

1. 2. They're dim-min' the street __

__ lights, you're per-fect for me. ____ Why aren't you here __ to-night? _____

30

would they write a song for you? ____

Mm, I can't help my - self, _

____ mm, mm, ____ my - self. ____

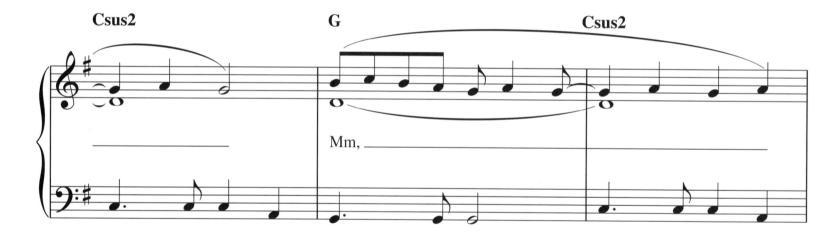

Mm, ____

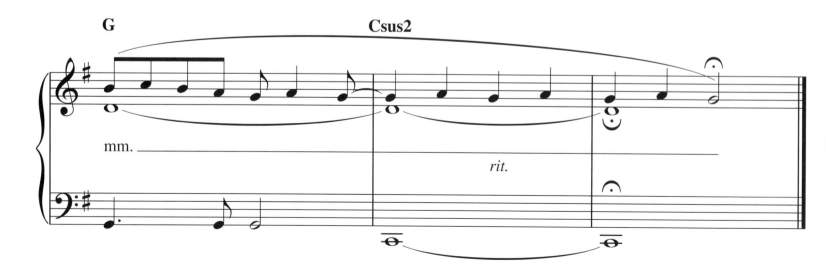

mm. ____

rit.

WHITE HORSE

Words and Music by TAYLOR SWIFT
and LIZ ROSE

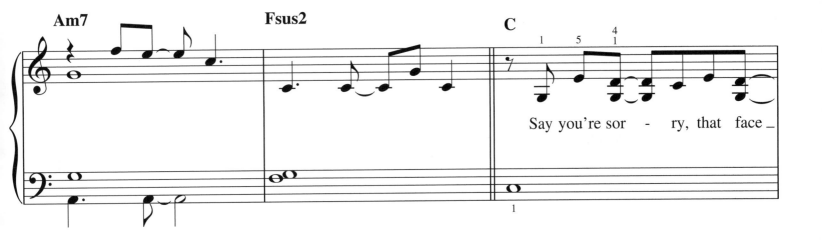

Say you're sor - ry, that face _

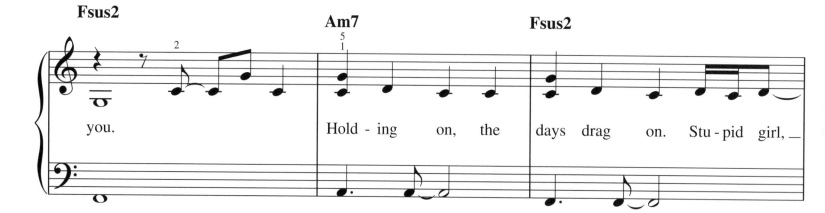

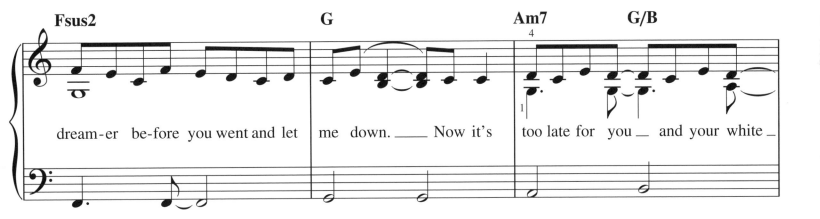

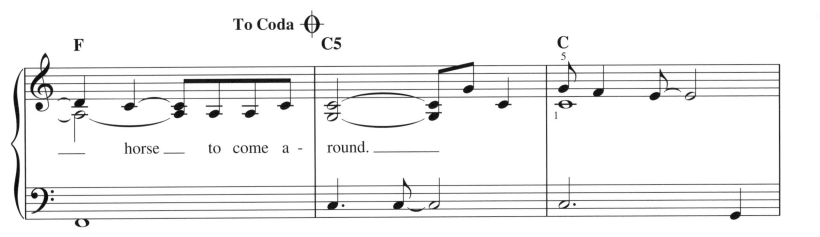

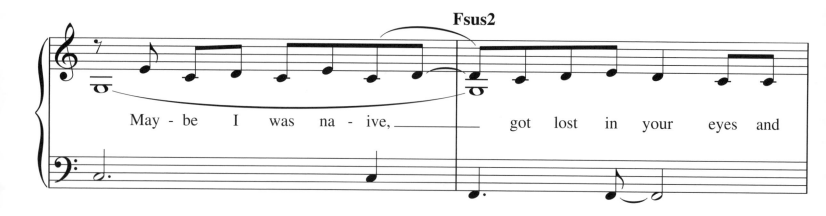

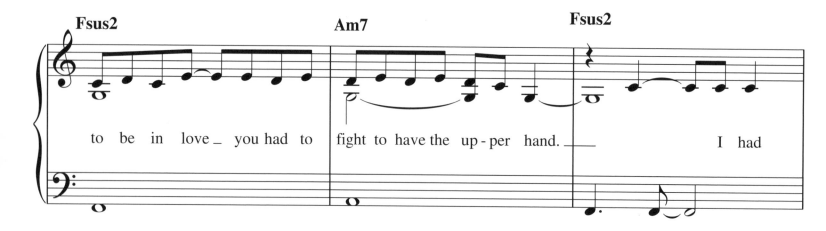

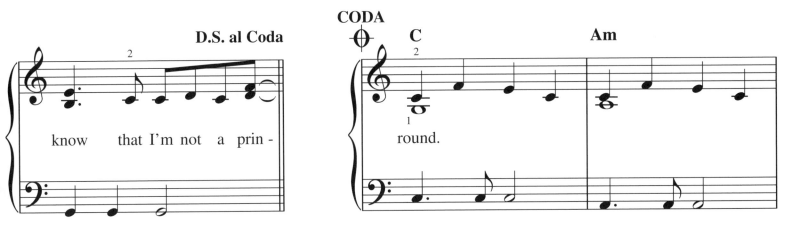

know   that I'm not a prin -

round.

And there you are   on your

knees,

beg-gin' for for-give-ness,

beg-gin' for me,

just like I al-ways want-ed,

but I'm   so

sor - ry. _____

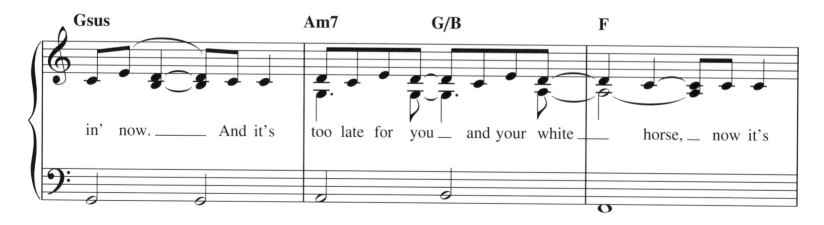

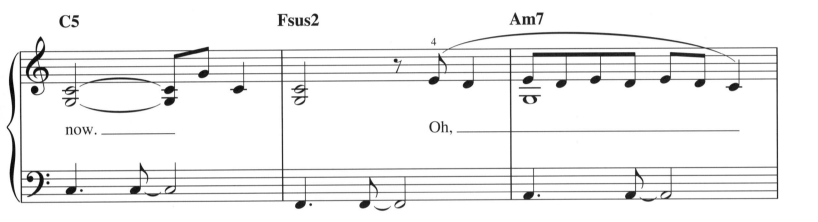

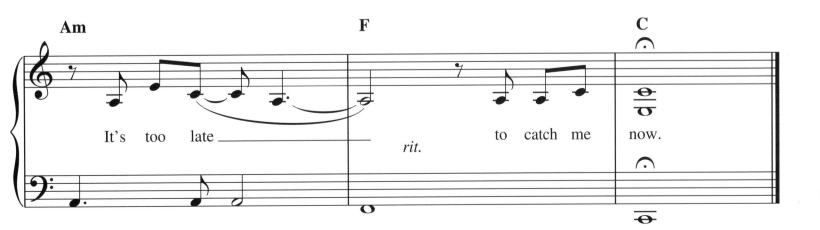

YOU BELONG WITH ME

Words and Music by TAYLOR SWIFT
and LIZ ROSE

Moderately fast

With pedal

1. You're on the phone with your girl-friend. She's up - set. __
2. *(See additional lyrics)*

__ She's go - in' off a - bout some - thin' that you said, __ 'cause she does - n't

get your hu - mor like I do.

G   D

I'm in the room, it's a typ-i-cal Tues-day night.___ I'm list-'nin' to the kind of

Am7

mu-sic she does-n't like.___ And she'll nev-er know your sto-ry like

C   Chorus
                      Am7

I do.   But she wears short skirts,
                               She wears high heels,

C   G   D

I wear T-shirts,
I wear sneak-ers,   she's cheer cap-tain and   I'm on the bleach-ers,

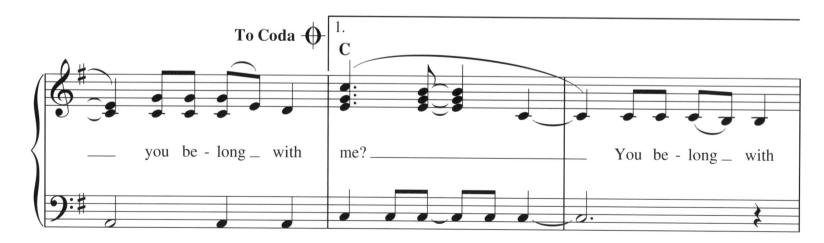

me.   me? _____

_____   Stand - ing by ___ and wait - ing at your back door.

All this time ___ how could ___ you not know, ba - by, _____

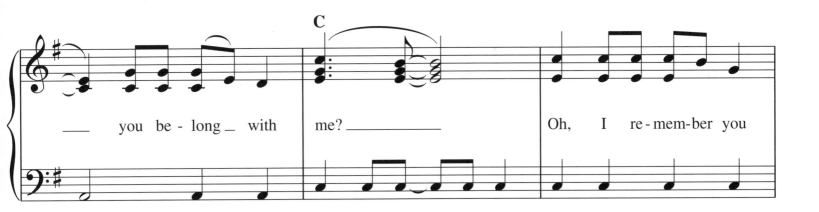

___ you be - long ___ with me? _____   Oh, I re - mem - ber you

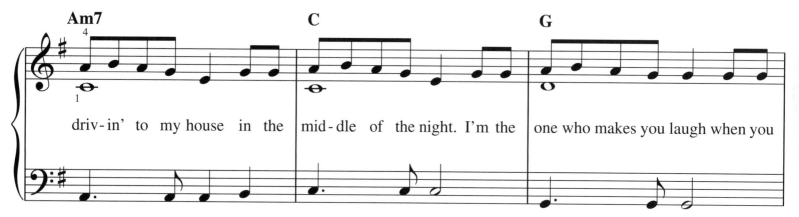

driv-in' to my house in the mid-dle of the night. I'm the one who makes you laugh when you

know you're 'bout to cry.   I know your fav-'rite songs and you tell me 'bout your dreams. Think I

know where you be-long. Think I know it's with   me. _____   Can't you

me? _____   Stand-in' by ___ here wait-

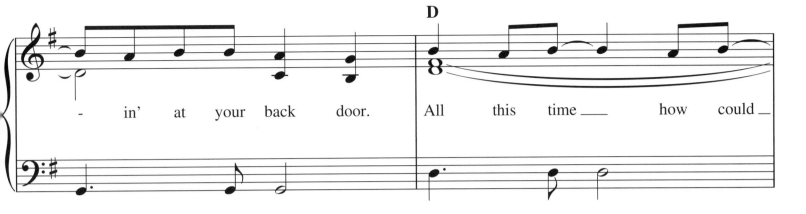

-in' at your back door. All this time ___ how could ___

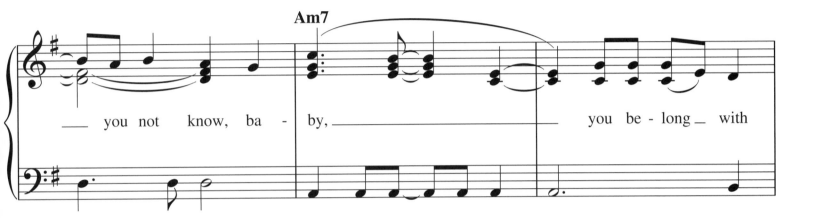

___ you not know, ba - by, ___ you be - long ___ with

me? ___ You be - long ___ with me.

Additional Lyrics

2. Walkin' the streets with you in your worn out jeans,
I can't help thinkin' this is how it ought to be.
Laughin' on a park bench, thinkin' to myself,
"Hey, isn't this easy?"
And you've got a smile that could light up this whole town.
I haven't seen it in a while since she brought you down.
You say you're fine. I know better than that.
Hey, what you doin' with a girl like that?
Chorus

BREATHE

Words and Music by TAYLOR SWIFT
and COLBIE CAILLAT

Moderately

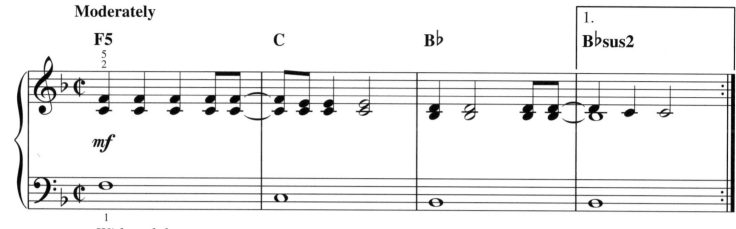

With pedal

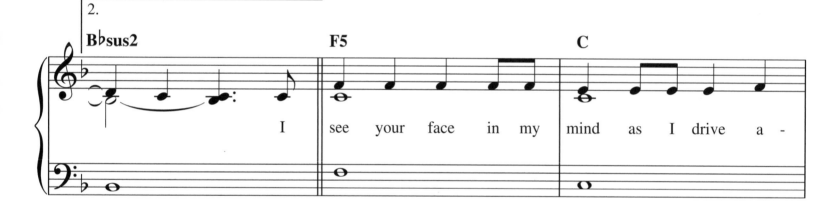

I see your face in my mind as I drive a-

way, 'cause none of us thought it was

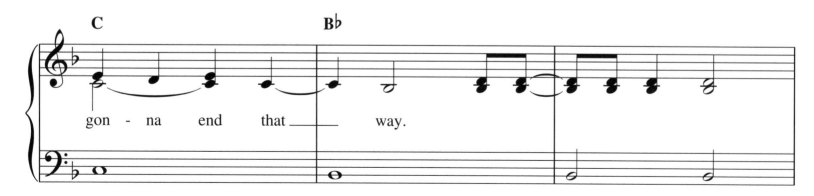

gon-na end that ___ way.

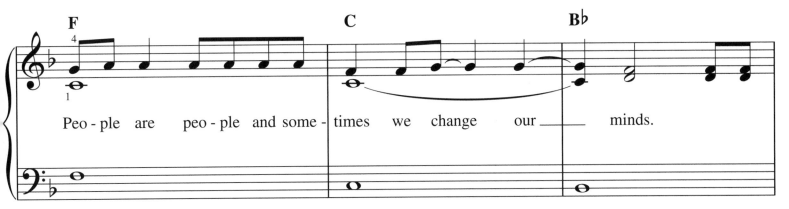

Peo - ple are peo - ple and some - times we change our _____ minds.

But it's kill - in' me to see you go af - ter all ___ this ___

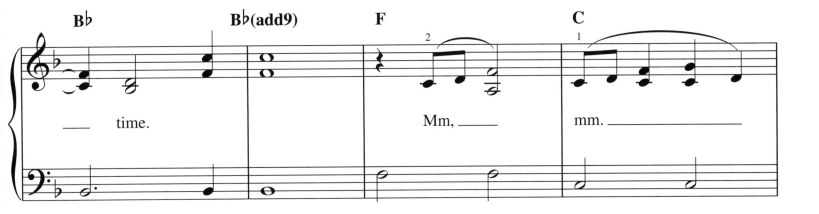

___ time. Mm, _____ mm. _____

Mm, ___ mm. _____

46

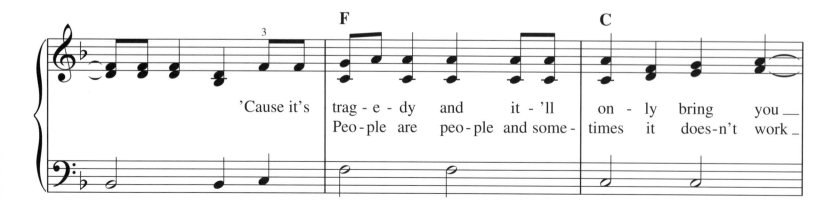

down.
out.

Now
And

I don't know what to
noth-in' we say is gon - na

be with-out you a -
save us from the fall -

round. _____
out. _____

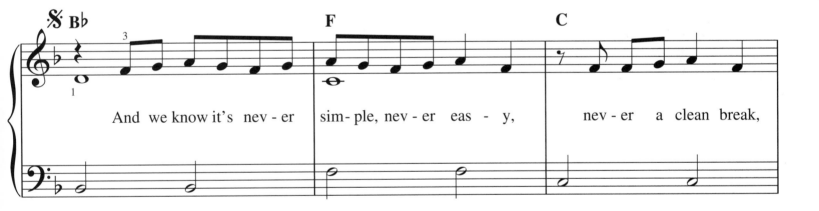

And we know it's nev - er

sim - ple, nev - er eas - y,

nev - er a clean break,

no one here to save me.

You're the on - ly thing I

know like the back of my

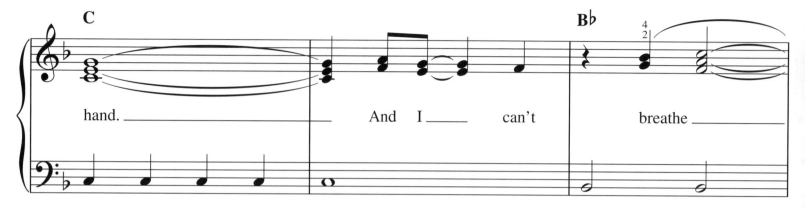

hand. _____ And I ____ can't breathe _____

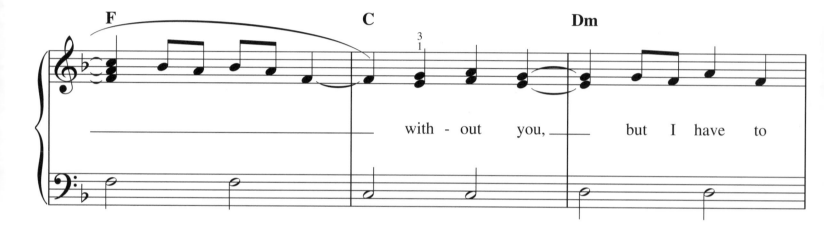

_____ with - out you, ____ but I have to

breathe _____ with - out you, ____

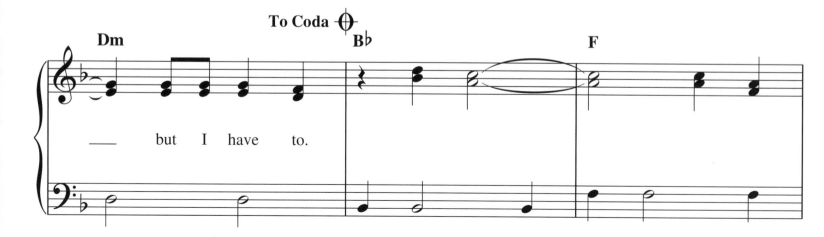

____ but I have to.

To Coda ⊕

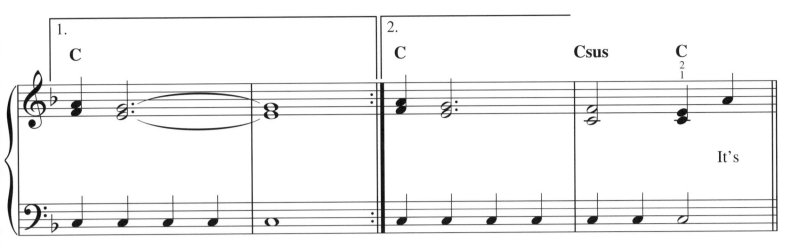

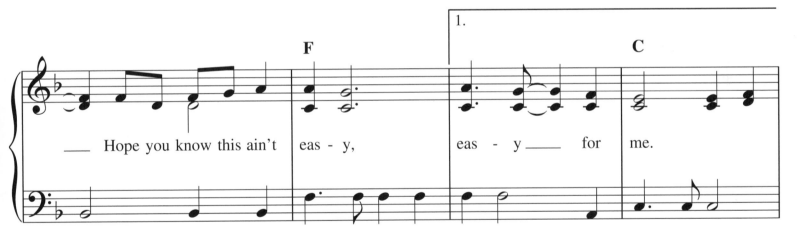

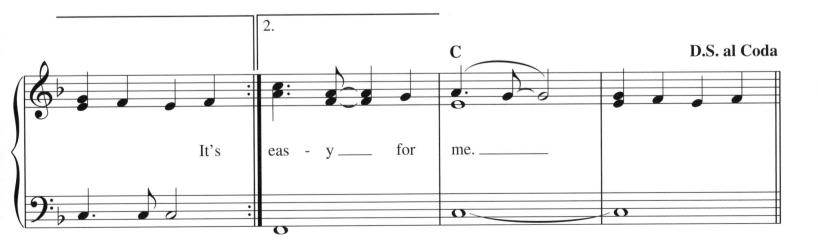

50

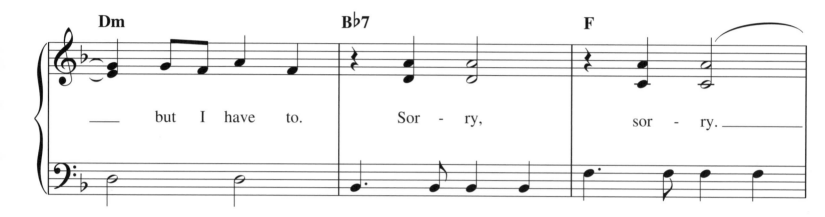

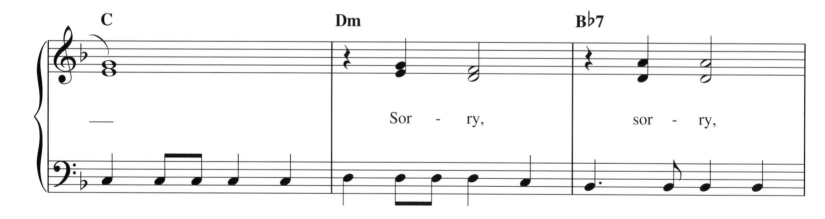

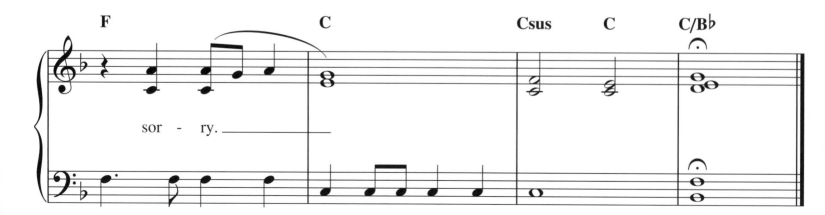

TELL ME WHY

Words and Music by TAYLOR SWIFT
and LIZ ROSE

Moderately fast, in 2

With pedal

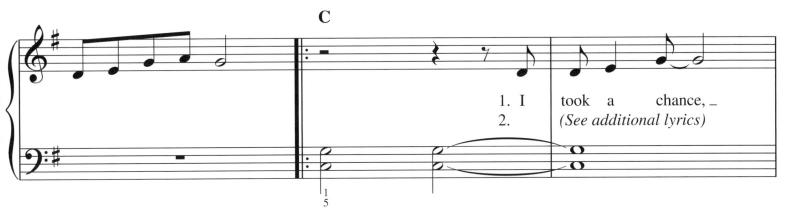

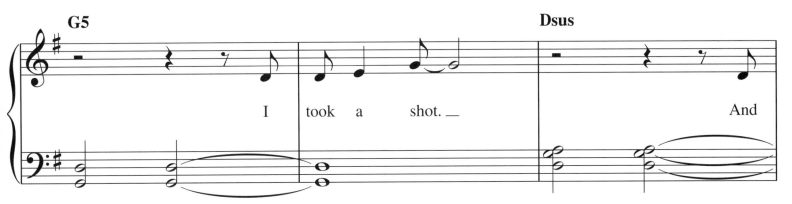

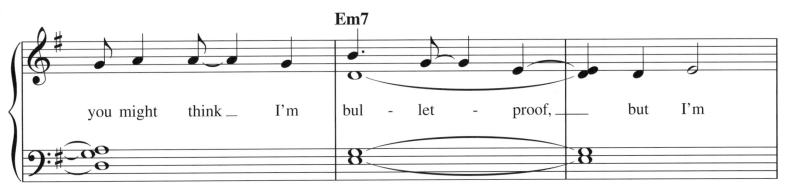

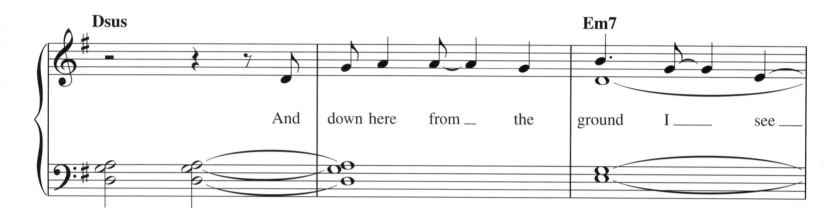

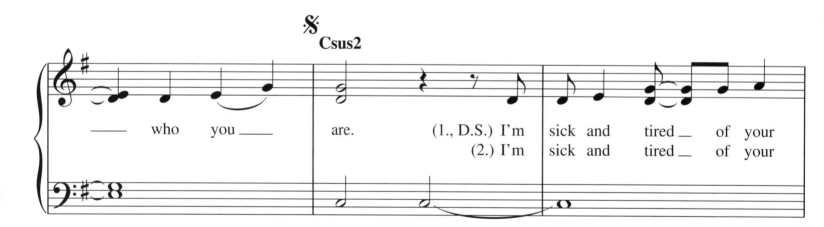

53

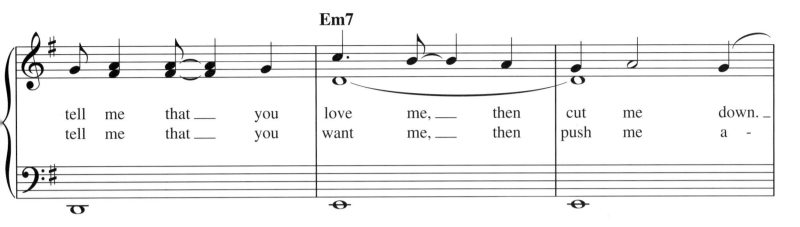

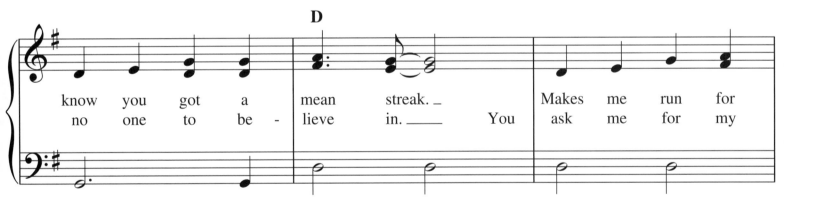

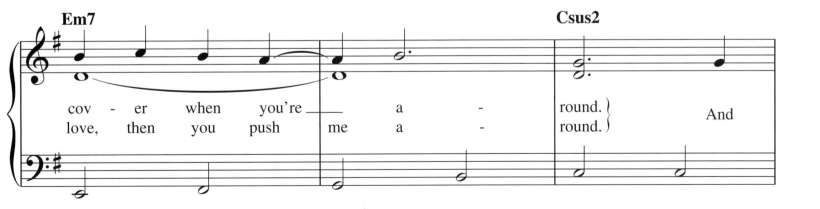

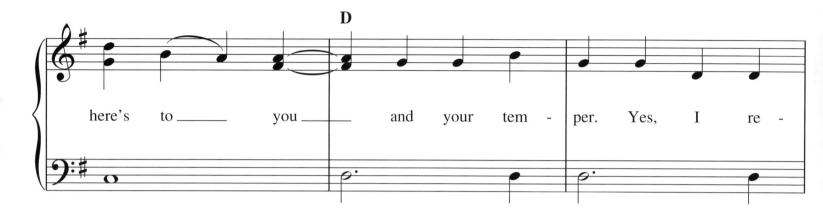

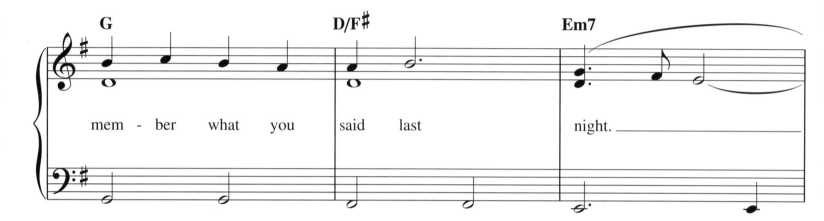

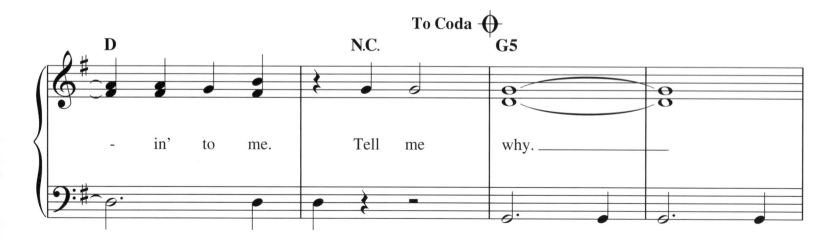

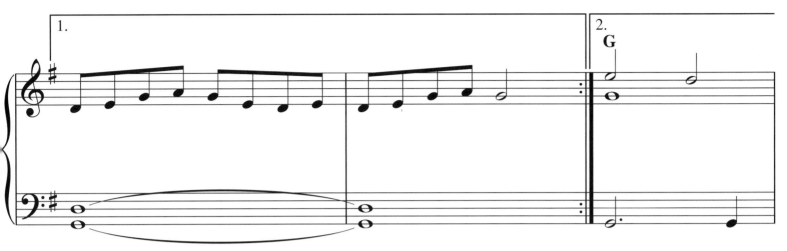

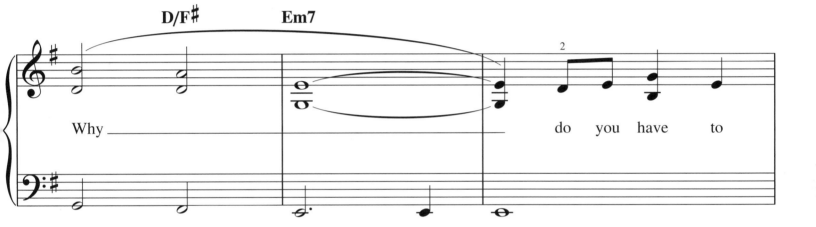

Why _____ do you have to

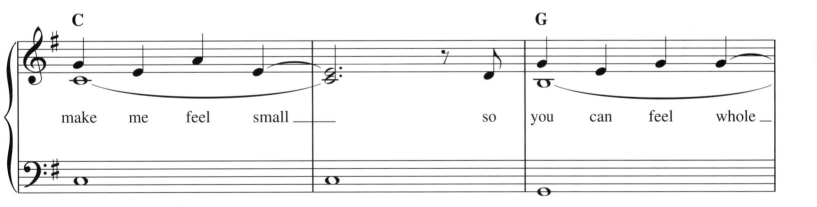

make me feel small _____ so you can feel whole ___

___ in - side? _____

56

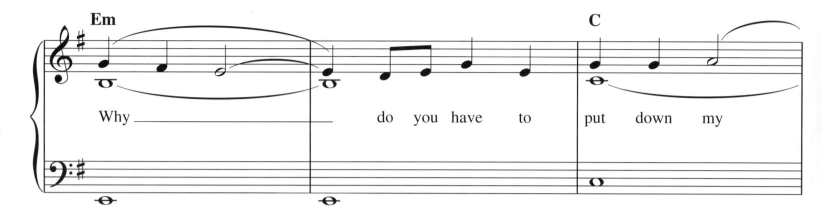

Why _____ do you have to put down my

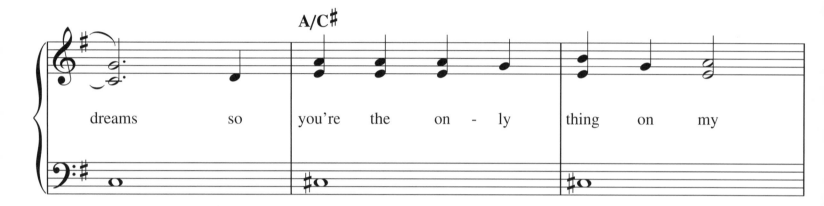

dreams so you're the on - ly thing on my

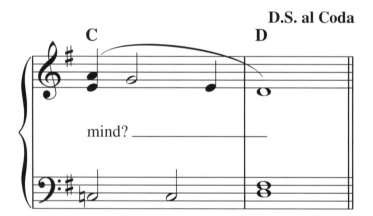

mind? _____ why. _____

Why, tell me why. _____

57

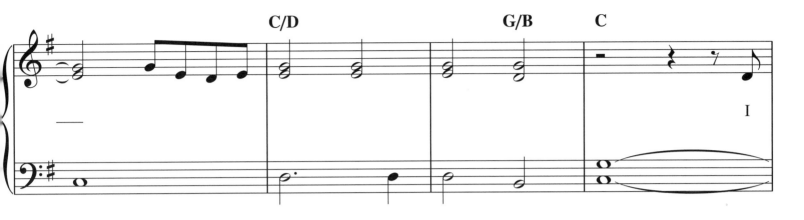

take a step back, let you go. I

told you I'm not bul - let - proof, now you know.

rit.

Additional Lyrics

2. You could write a book on how
To ruin someone's perfect day.
Well, I get so confused and frustrated,
Forget what I'm tryin' to say. Oh...

I'm sick and tired...

YOU'RE NOT SORRY

Words and Music by
TAYLOR SWIFT

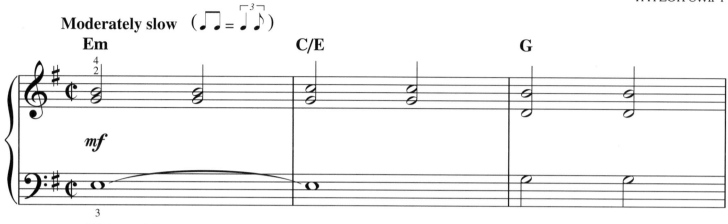

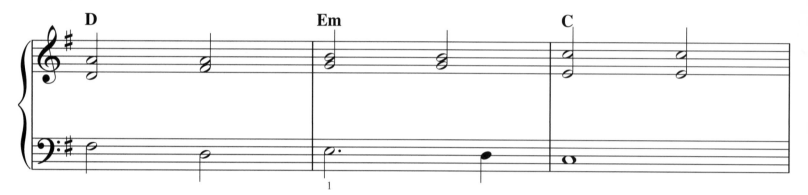

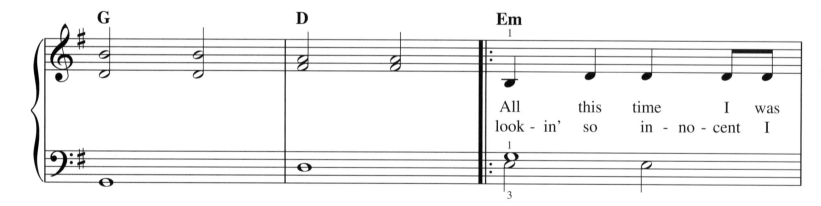

Lyrics:

All this time I was wast-in', hop-in' you would come a-round. I've been

look-in' so in-no-cent I might be-lieve you if I did-n't know. Could-'ve

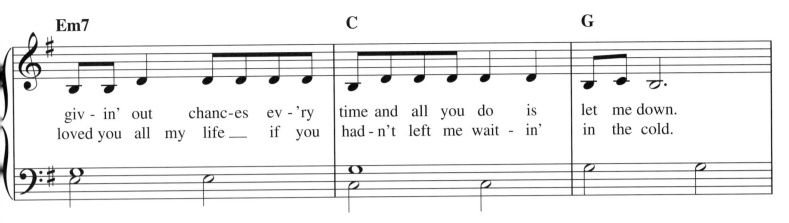

giv - in' out   chanc-es   ev -'ry | time and all you do   is | let me down.
loved you all my life __ if you | had-n't left me wait - in' | in the cold.

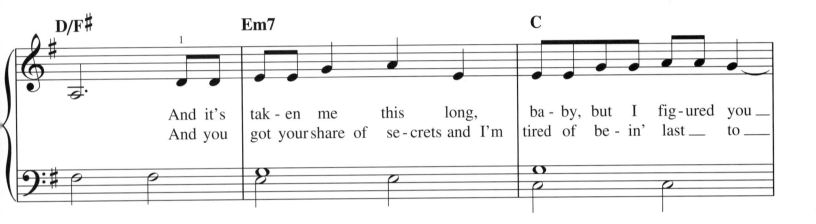

And it's | tak - en me   this   long, | ba - by, but I fig-ured you __
And you | got your share of se-crets and I'm | tired of be - in' last __ to __

__ out. | | And you're |think- in' we'll be fine a - gain, but
__ know. | | And now you're |ask - in' me to list - en 'cause it's

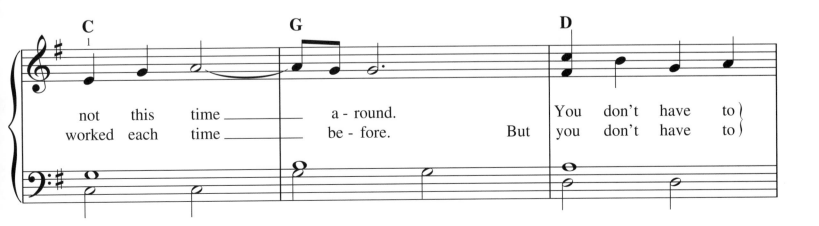

not   this   time _____   a - round. | You don't have   to)
worked each time _____   be - fore. | But | you don't have   to)

call _____ an - y - more. I won't pick up the phone. _____

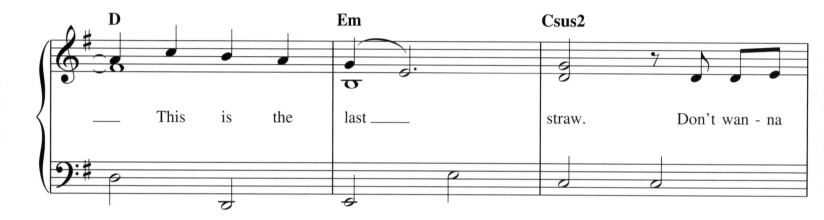

_____ This is the last _____ straw. Don't wan - na

hurt an - y - more. _____ And you can tell me that you're sor - ry, but I

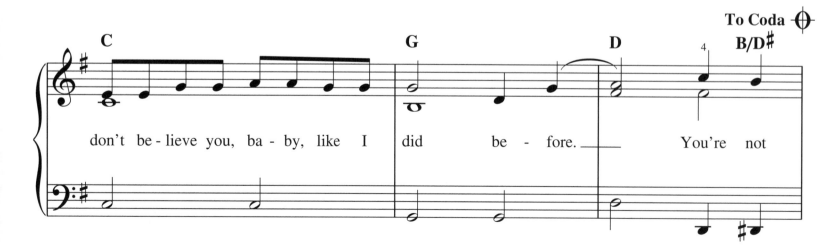

don't be - lieve you, ba - by, like I did be - fore. _____ You're not

61

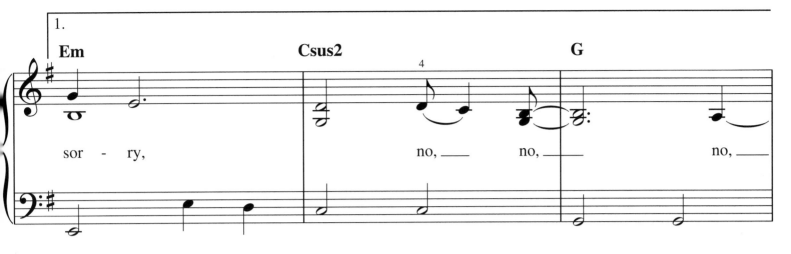

sor - ry, no, ___ no, ___ no, ___

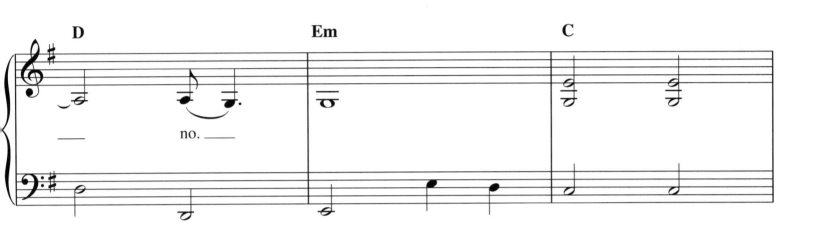

no. ___

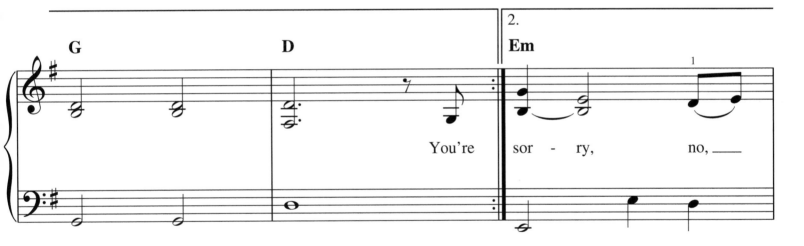

You're sor - ry, no, ___

no. _____ You're not

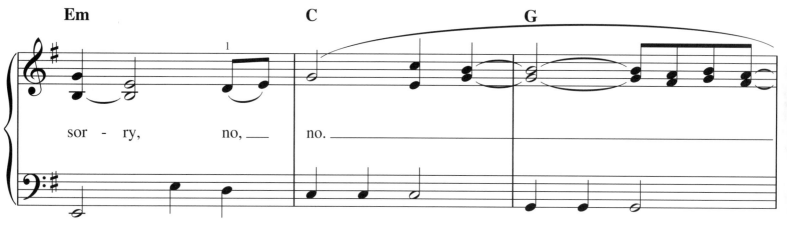

sor - ry, no, ___ no. ___

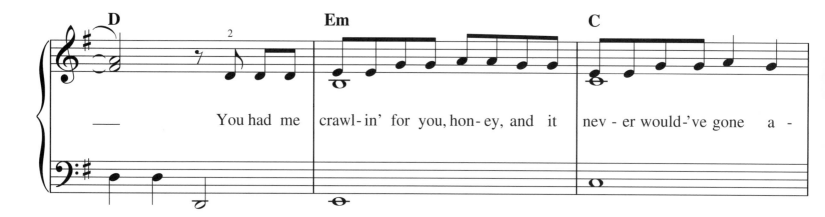

___ You had me crawl-in' for you, hon-ey, and it nev - er would-'ve gone a -

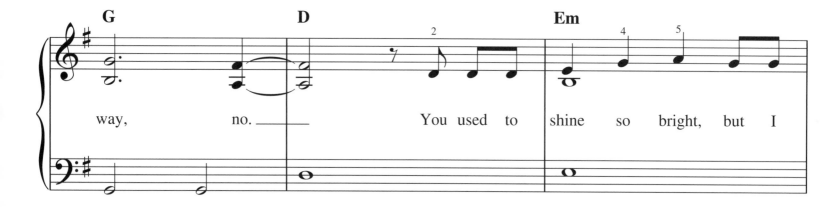

way, no. ___ You used to shine so bright, but I

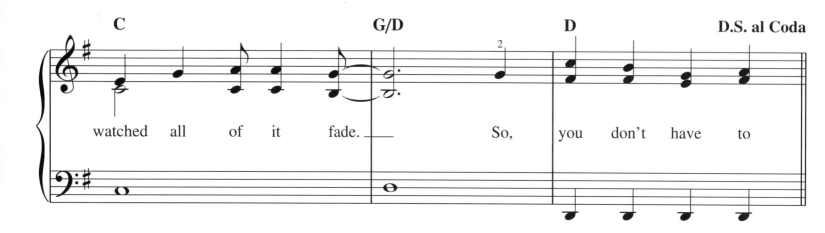

watched all of it fade. ___ So, you don't have to

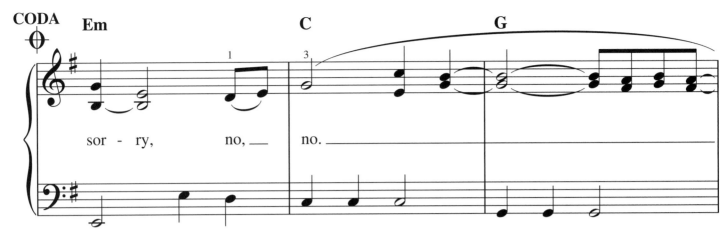

sor - ry, no, — no.

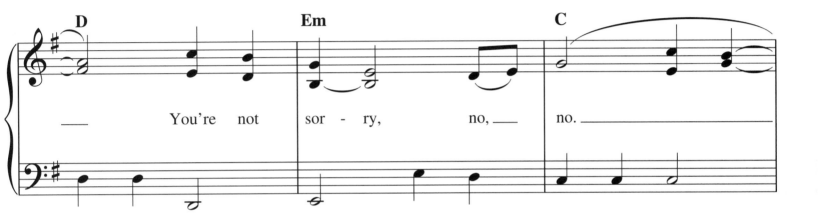

— You're not sor - ry, no, — no.

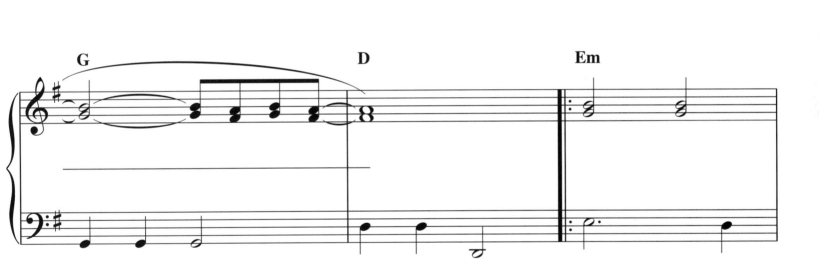

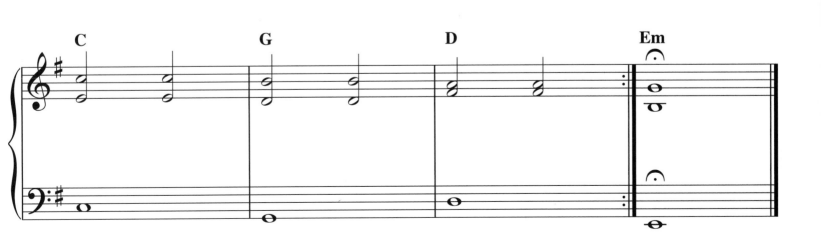

THE WAY I LOVED YOU

Words and Music by TAYLOR SWIFT
and JOHN RICH

Moderately slow

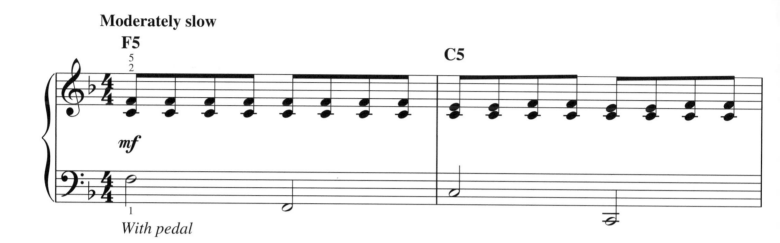

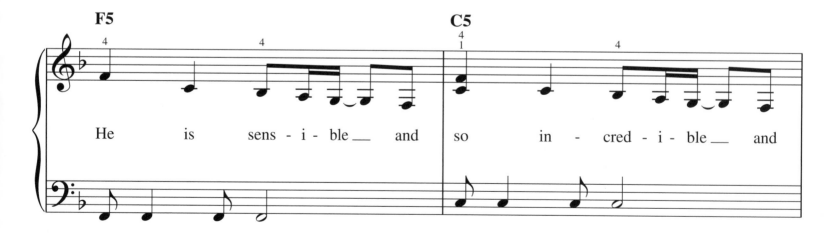

He is sens - i - ble __ and so in - cred - i - ble __ and

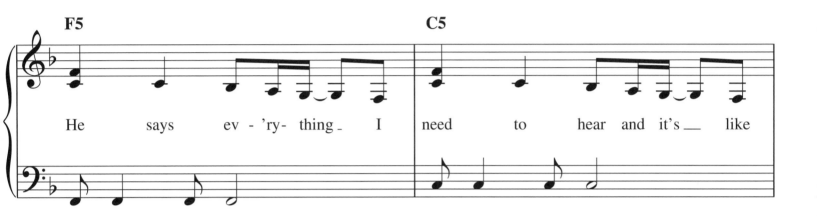

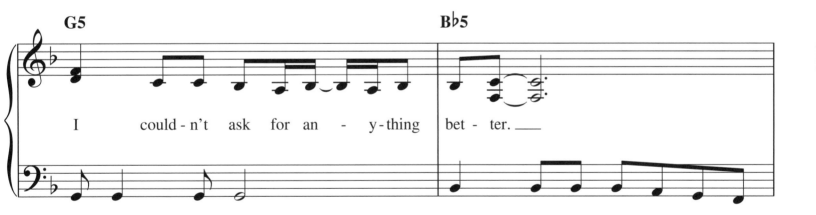

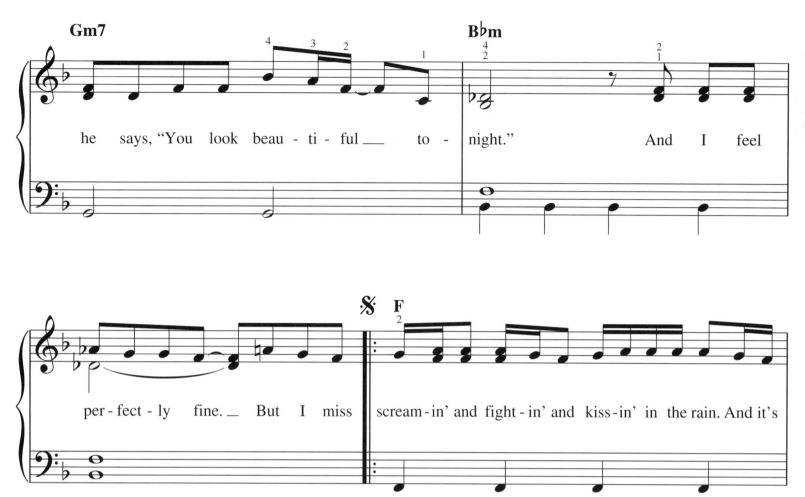

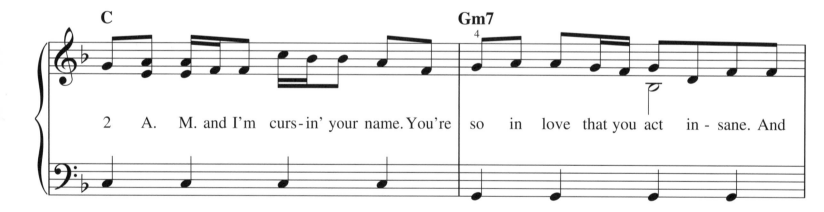

C **Gm7** **To Coda**

rol - ler - coast - er kind of rush. And I nev - er knew I could feel that much and

B♭ **B♭m** **C**

that's the way I loved you. _____

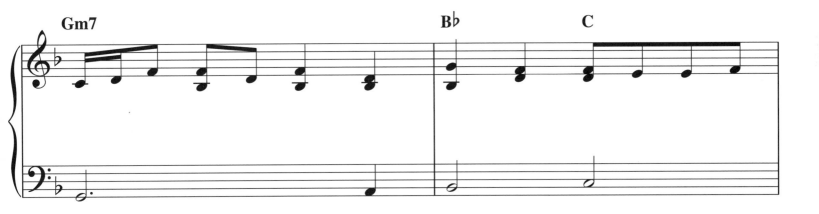

Gm7 **B♭** **C**

1.

F **Csus**

He re - spects my space and nev - er makes me wait _ and

68

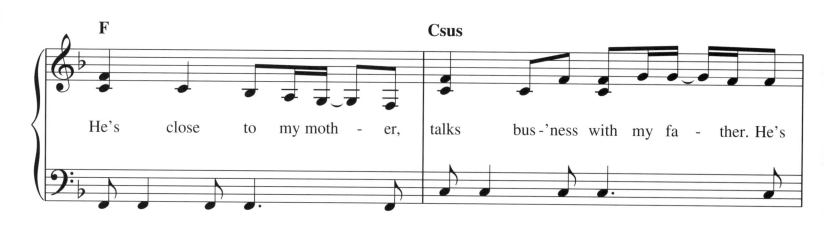

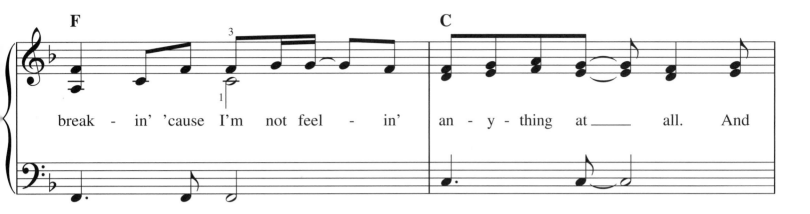

break - in' 'cause I'm not feel - in' an - y - thing at _____ all. And

you were wild and cra - zy, just so frus - tr - at - ing, in -

tox - i - cat - ing, com - pli - cat - ed. Got a - way by some mis - take, and

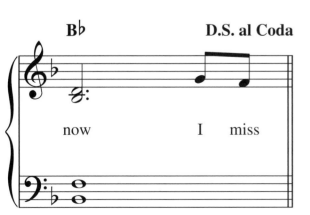

now I miss

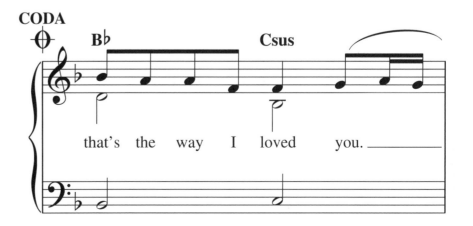

that's the way I loved you. _____

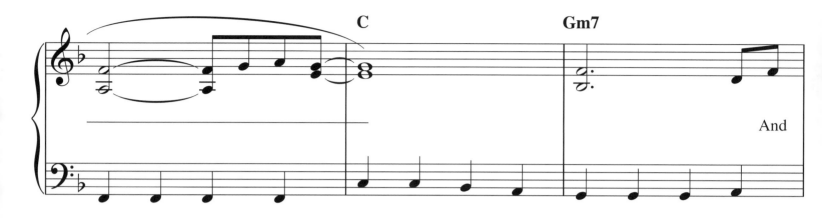

CHANGE

Words and Music by
TAYLOR SWIFT

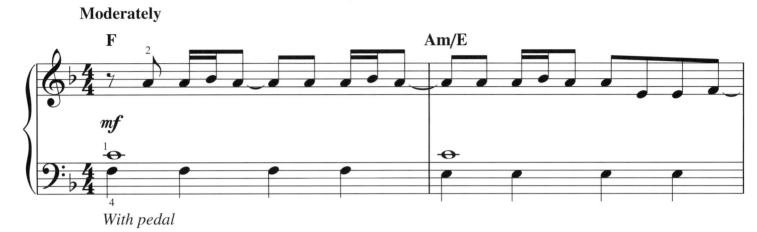

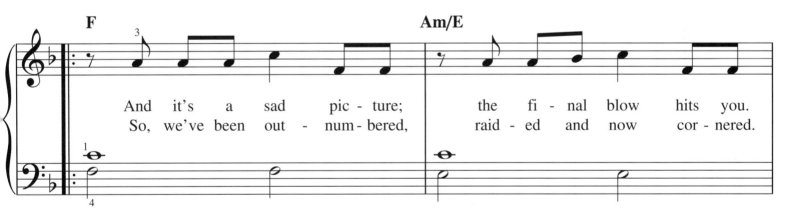

And it's a sad pic-ture; the fi-nal blow hits you.
So, we've been out-num-bered, raid-ed and now cor-nered.

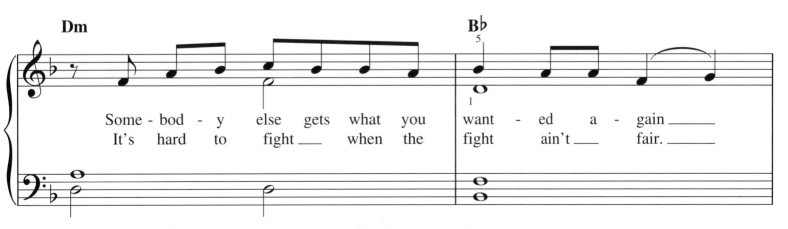

Some-bod-y else gets what you want-ed a-gain ___
It's hard to fight ___ when the fight ain't ___ fair. ___

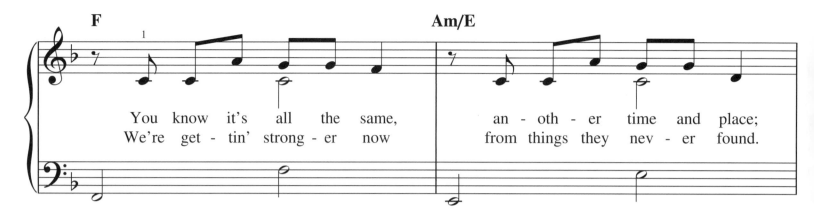

You know it's all the same, an - oth - er time and place;
We're get - tin' strong - er now from things they nev - er found.

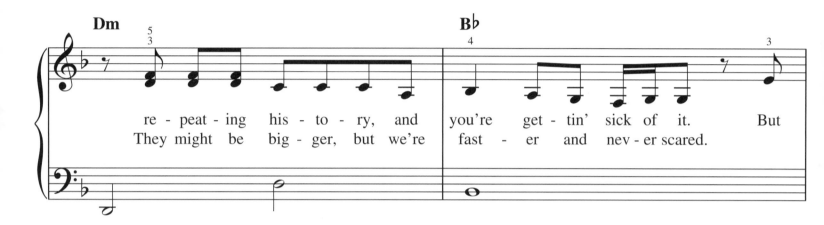

re - peat - ing his - to - ry, and you're get - tin' sick of it. But
They might be big - ger, but we're fast - er and nev - er scared.

I be - lieve in what - ev - er you do. And I'll do
You can walk a - way, say we don't need this. But there's __

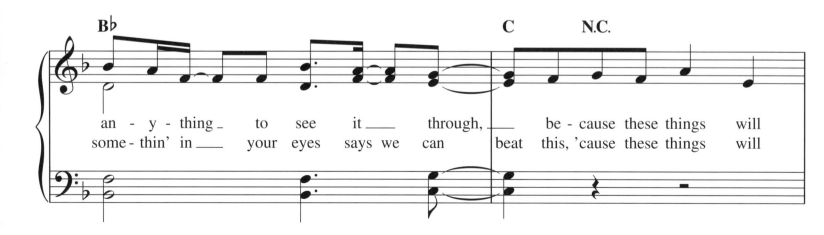

an - y - thing __ to see it __ through, __ be - cause these things will
some - thin' in __ your eyes says we can beat this, 'cause these things will

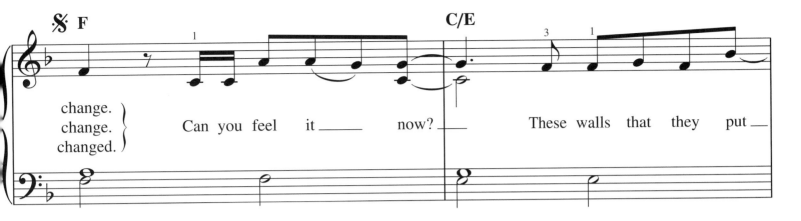

change.
change.
changed.
Can you feel it ____ now? ____ These walls that they put ____

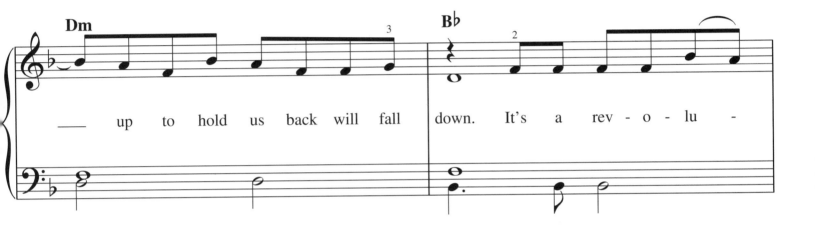

____ up to hold us back will fall down. It's a rev - o - lu -

tion. ((1.,2.) The time will come ____ for us to fi - nal - ly win. ____
(D.S.) Throw your hands up, ____ 'cause we nev - er gave in. ____

And we'll sing hal - le - lu - jah, ____ we'll sing hal - le - lu -

To - night _ we'll stand _ and get off _ our knees, _ fight for what _ we've

worked for _ all _ these years. And the bat-tle was long. _ It's the fight _ of our lives, _

but we'll stand __ up cham-pions to-night.

It was the night things

D.S. al Coda

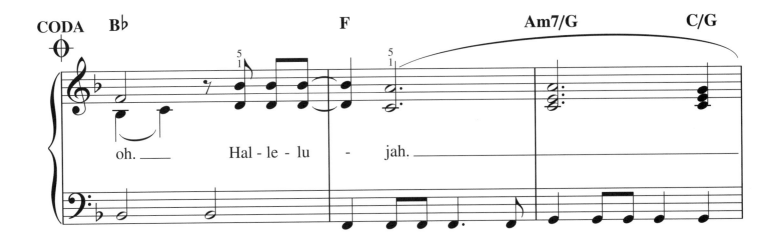

CODA B♭ F Am7/G C/G

oh. ___ Hal - le - lu - jah. ___

Dm/A B♭ F/C

C Dm B♭

rit.

FOREVER & ALWAYS

Words and Music by
TAYLOR SWIFT

Moderately fast

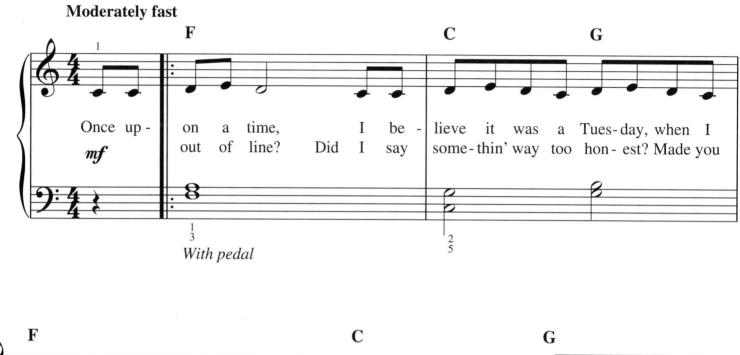

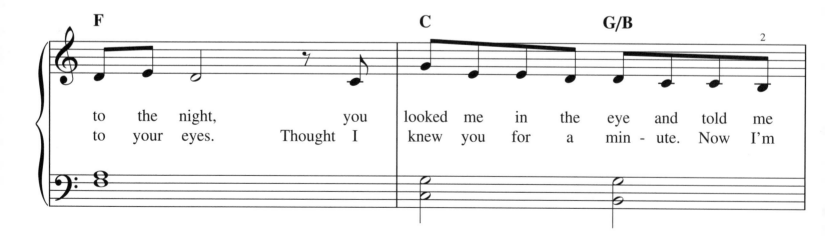

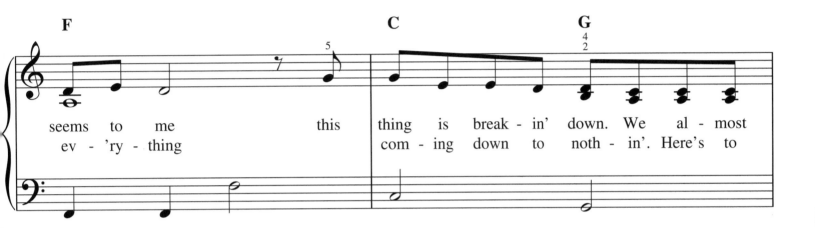

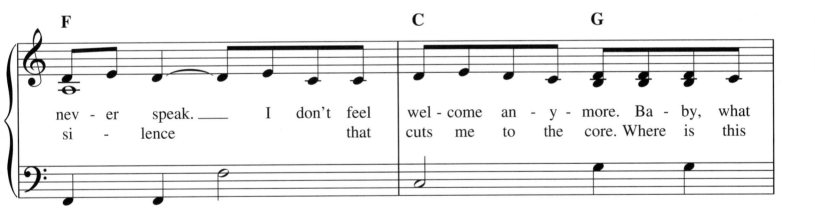

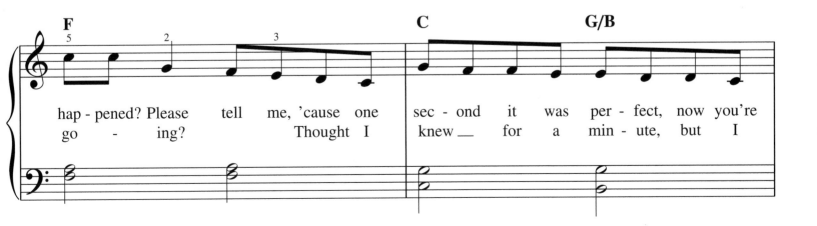

F **G** **𝄋 F**

half - way out the door. ____

don't ____ an - y - more. ____ And I ____ stare at the phone. He still

C **G**

has - n't { (1.,2.) called ____ and then }

{ (D.S.) called ____ me. Then } you feel so low you can't

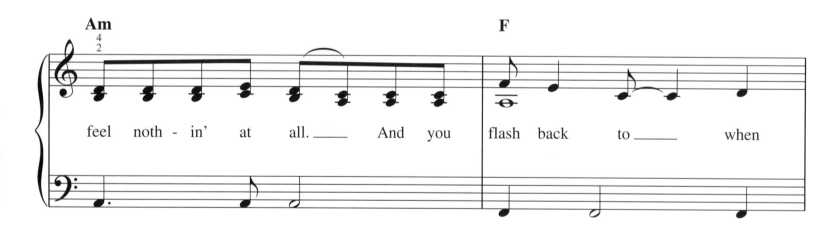

Am **F**

feel noth - in' at all. ____ And you flash back to ____ when

C/E **G**

{ he }

{ we } said, "for - ev - er and al - ways." Oh, ____ oh ____ and it

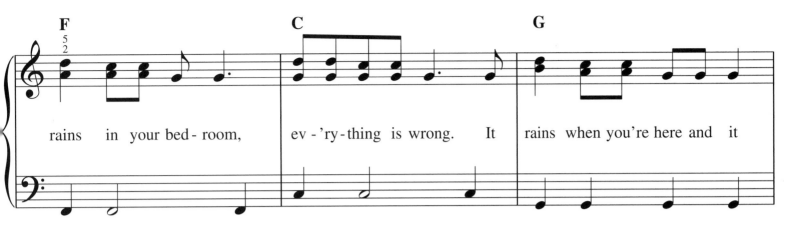

rains in your bed-room, ev-'ry-thing is wrong. It rains when you're here and it

rains when you're gone. 'Cause I was there __ when you said "for-ev-er and

al-ways." Was I You did-n't mean it, ba-by.

I don't think so.

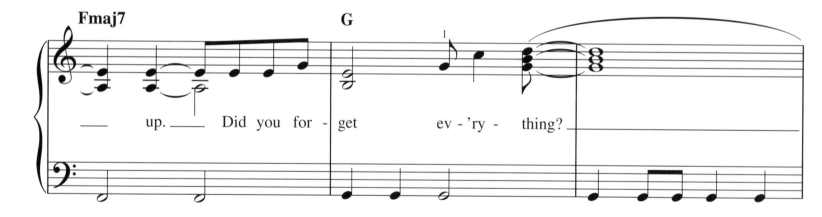

81

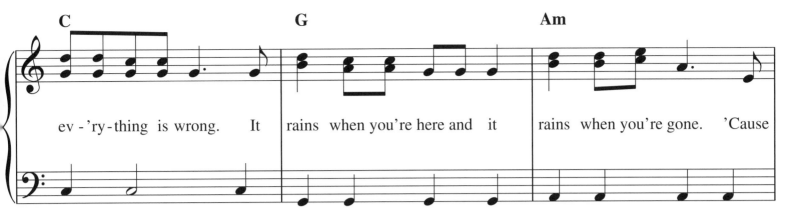

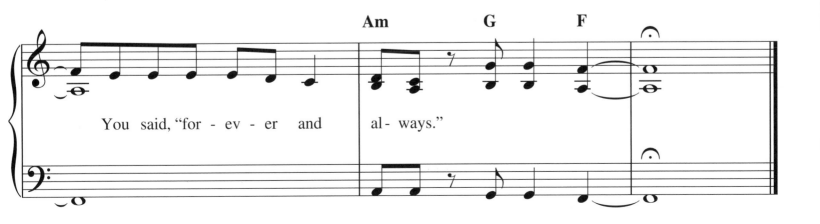

THE BEST DAY

Words and Music by
TAYLOR SWIFT

Moderately

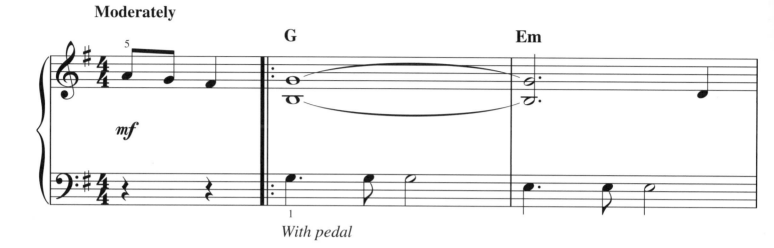

With pedal

I'm five ___ years
I'm thir - teen
There is ___ a

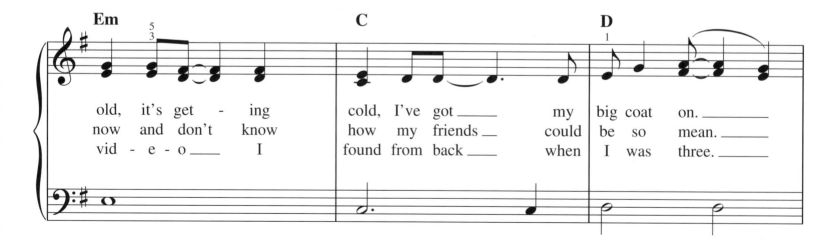

old, it's get - ing ... cold, I've got ___ my big coat on. ___
now and don't know ... how my friends ___ could be so mean. ___
vid - e - o ___ I ... found from back ___ when I was three. ___

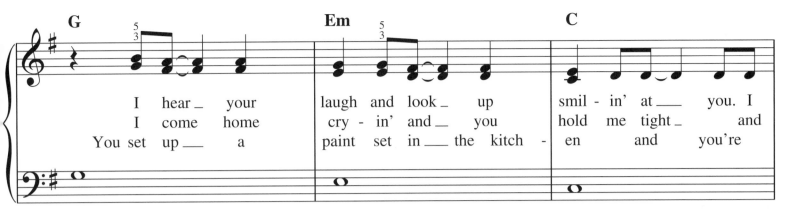

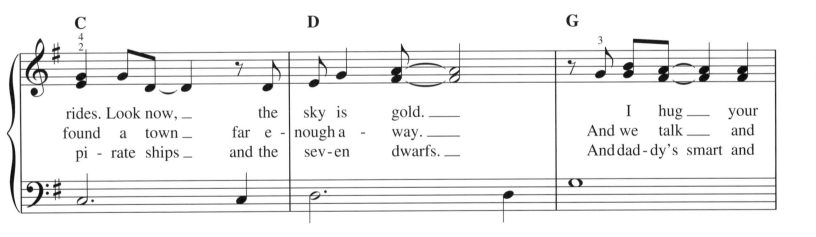

C   **D**   **G**   **D/F#**

I don't _ know _ why   all   the   trees change   in   the
I don't _ know _ who   I'm gon - na   talk   to   now   at
Now I _____ know _ why   all   the   trees change   in   the

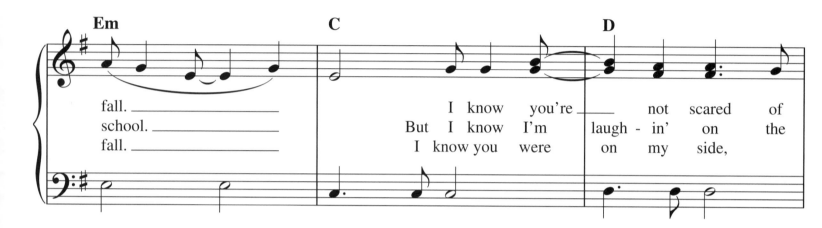

Em   **C**   **D**

fall. _____   I know you're _ not scared of
school. _____   But I know I'm   laugh - in' on   the
fall. _____   I know you were   on   my   side,

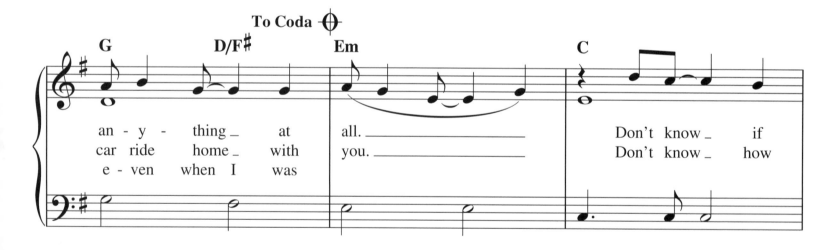

To Coda ⊕

G   **D/F#**   **Em**   **C**

an - y - thing _ at   all. _____   Don't know _ if
car ride home _ with   you. _____   Don't know _ how
e - ven when I was

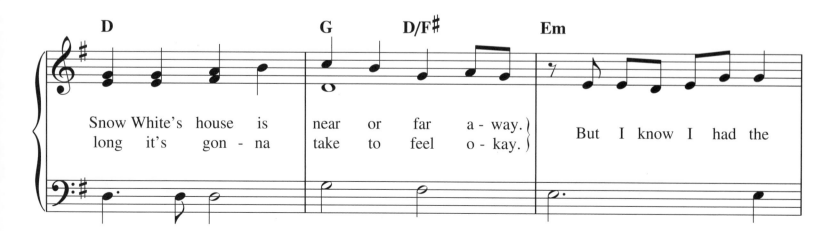

D   **G**   **D/F#**   **Em**

Snow White's house is   near or far a - way. ⎫
long it's gon - na   take to feel o - kay. ⎭   But I know I had the

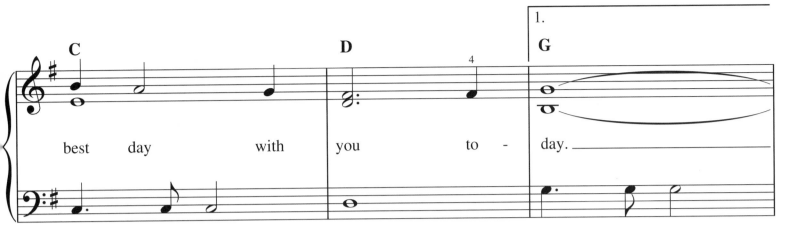

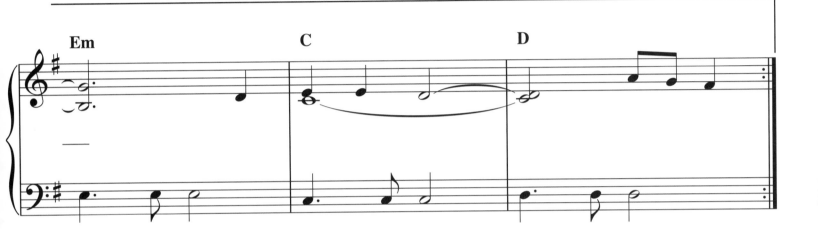

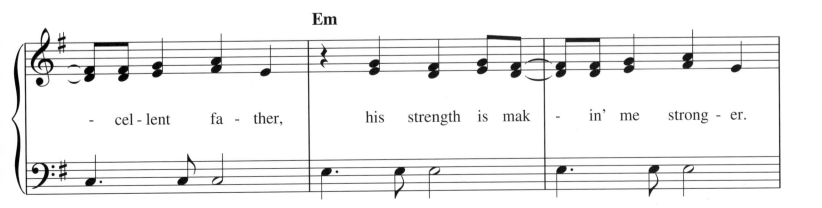

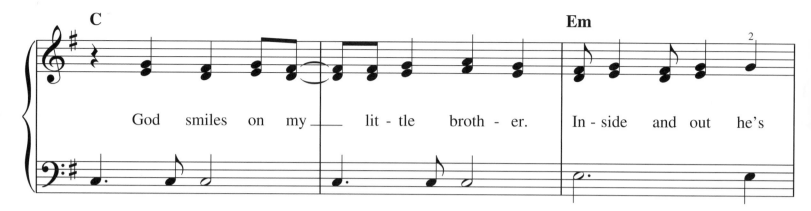

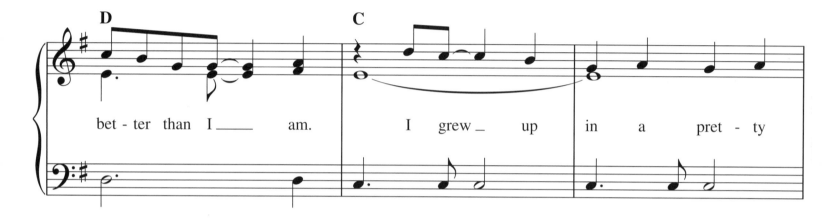

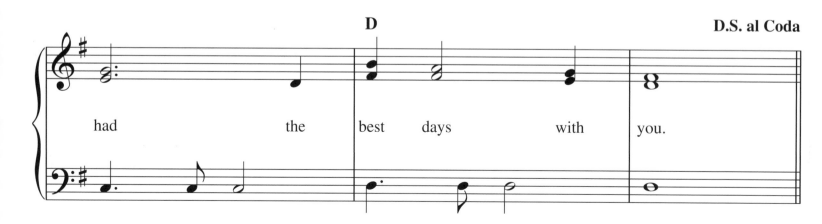

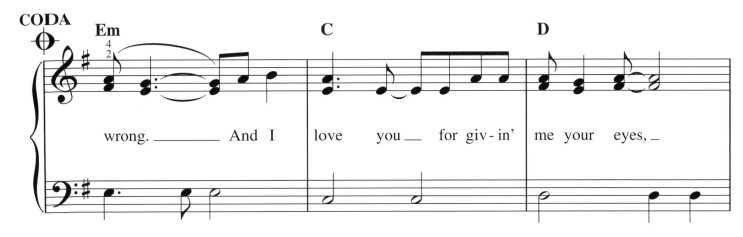

wrong. _____ And I love you _ for giv-in' me your eyes, _

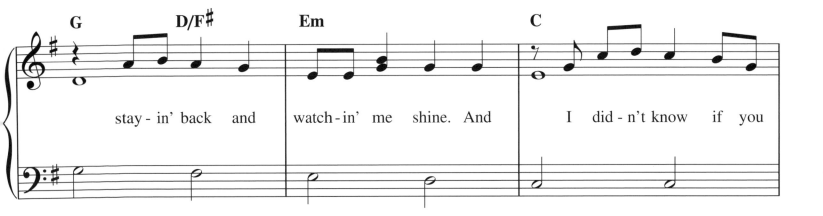

stay-in' back and watch-in' me shine. And I did-n't know if you

knew, so I'm tak-in' this chance to say that I had the

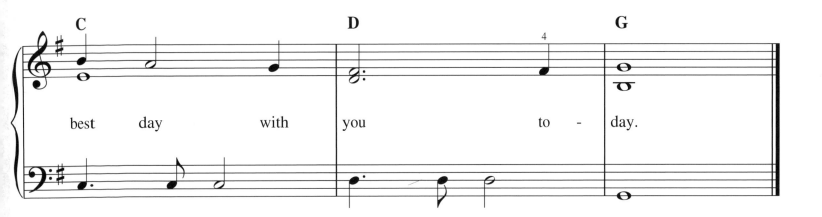

best day with you to-day.